Healthy Lifestyle Recipes Publishing
HLR Press
Southern California

Our Complete Hamilton Beach® Ice Cream Recipe Book

Hamilton Beach® is a subsidiary of diversified conglomerate NACCO Industries and is known worldwide for being one of the top appliance brand producers in the industries, in my opinion. Most products by Hamilton Beach® are sold through wholesale distributors and or retailers in North America. The company has roots tracing back to 1904 and is still one of the top in its industry of products and appliances today! Healthy Lifestyle Recipes and Samantha Kaine are not affiliated with Hamilton Beach®. All material in this book are only the views and opinions of the author.

LEGAL NOTICE

This information contained in this book is for entertainment purposes only. No part of this book, in any way shape or form, may be reproduced or transmitted in any form by any means whatsoever without express written permission from the author, except in the case of brief quotations embodied in critical articles and reviews. The content represents the opinion of the author and is based on the author's personal experience and observations. The author or the company does not assume any liability whatsoever for the use of or inability to use any or all information contained in this book, and accepts no responsibility for any loss or damages of any kind that may be incurred by the reader as a result of actions arising from the use of the information in this book. Use this information at your own risk.

The author reserves the right to make any changes he or she deems necessary to future versions of the publication to ensure its accuracy.

COPYRIGHT © 2017 Healthy Lifestyle Recipes

All rights reserved.

Published in the United States of America by Healthy Lifestyle Recipes

www.HealthyLifestyleRecipes.org

WANT FREE BOOKS?
... OF COURSE YOU DO!

Our New Books Sent To Your Email Monthly

For our current readers...if you like receiving FREE Books to add to your collection, then this is for you! This is for promoting our material to our current members so you can review our new books and give us feed back when we launch new books we are publishing! This helps us determine how we can make our books better for YOU, our audience! Just go to the url below and leave your name and email. We will send you a complimentary book about once a month. And just an FYI...on the website we've posted a few videos for you here too...

The Waffle Cone Recipe
Yours FREE for signing up to Our List!

www.HealthyLifestyleRecipes.org/FreeBook2Review

INTRODUCTION

Homemade Ice Cream Any Way You Want...Anytime You Can Get It!

Prepared to be "Wow'd" by these "Top of the Line" Ice Cream Recipes that will have you creating ice cream flavors you could only imagine could be made!

If You Are Craving Something Sweet, Then We've Got Some Great Tasting Flavors of Ice Cream, Frozen Yogurt, Milkshake, Gelato & Sorbets that You Can Make Any Way You Want, Right at Home! Indulge yourself in these amazing flavors that will having your craving ice cream every day of the week! We have packed over 100 recipes inside of this wonderful book for you to cherish for a very long time. Everyone will love the new your of the ice cream world! And don't forget that you can also whip up some those fun Frozen Yogurt, Gelato, Custard, Sorbet and Milkshakes! And remember...It's more fun when you share! ;)

We show you how to make every kind of frozen dessert you can get out of this machine by starting you out with "The Classics", Then we get "Fruitilicious", and show you "Something Different", then walk you "On the Healthy Side", Then we give you a section for those "Kiddos" by introducing our special section called "Childs Play" and last but not least..."Grown Ups Only!" So this book is for everyone young and old!

We've even got a little special something for the Adults! "Our Adult Section" is packed with the following...Double Gin And Tonic Soft Serve Ice Cream, Margarita Madness Soft Serve Ice Cream, Vanilla Screwdriver Soft Serve Ice Cream, "Adults Old Fashioned" Ice Cream, "New York" Manhattan Ice Cream and Creamy Kahlua Almond Delight Ice Cream!

Start turning these pages and dive right in! Your "Ice Creamin" journey is about to begin...**and may the scoop be with you!**
Enjoy! xoxo ~Samantha Kaine!

Our Complete Hamilton Beach® Ice Cream Recipe Book

Table of Contents

Want Free Books? ... Of Course You Do! 4
Our New Books Sent To Your Email Monthly 4

Introduction 5

Accessorizing Your Ice Cream 12
Start With A Base For Your Ice Cream 12
Toppings 13
Don't Forget The Sauce 14

Chapter 1: 15
Why This Book Is A Must!
The Only Ice Cream Maker Book For All Your Indulgences! 15
Sculpt Your Scoops! The Art Of Frozen Yogurt, Ice Cream, & Sorbet 16
31 Flavors??? Try 99! 17
Master The Craft! 18
The Possibilities Are Endless! 19

Chapter 2: 20
This Ice Cream Maker Will Change The Life Of Your Dessert World!
The Dessert That Goes With Everything! 20
The Old 31 Flavors Is A Thing Of The Past... 21
What's Not To Enjoy About Ice Cream? 21
Strong As An Igloo! 22
Safe, Sensible, & Smart! 23

Chapter 3: 24
Benefits Of This Frozen Yogurt, Sorbet And Ice Cream Maker!
Make Any Flavored Ice Cream You Want! 24
We've Got More Colors Than Crayola! 25
The Best Of The Best! 26
Cleaning Is Just As Easy! 27

Chapter 4:   28
There's More Than Ice Cream On The Menu!
What Else Is There To Make?   28
Look Beyond The Cone…   29
Make It Sinfully Delicious!   30
I Scream, You Scream, We All Scream For Ice Cream… And More!   31

Chapter 5:   32
How To Use Your Ice Cream Maker!
Easy As 1-2-3   32

The Steps   33
There's More To It!   34
Presentation Is Always A Must!   35

Chapter 6:   37
Things The Pros Know!
You Don't Have To Feel So Guilty!   37
Be An Inventor… Create That Ice Cream Dream!   38

Chapter 7:   39
Storage For Later!
Captain Obvious Says, "Keep It Cold."   39
Channel Your Inner Tetris   40
Destroy The Evidence!   40
Satisfy The Sweet Tooth!   41

The Classics   42
Classic Vanilla Soft-Serve Ice Cream   42
Chunky Chocolate Chip Soft Serve Ice Cream   44
California Cookies-N-Cream Soft Serve Ice Cream   45
Radical Rocky Road Ice Cream   46
Miraculous Double Mint Chip Ice Cream   47
Power Punch Pistachio Ice Cream   48
Double Dark Chocolate Gelato   49
Very Strawberry Gelato   50
Chocolate Chip Cookie Dough Frozen Yogurt   51
Divine Coffee Frozen Yogurt   52
Pralines And "Oh So Creamy" Milkshake   53
Mint Cookies 'N Cream "Silkshake"   54

Fruitilicious — 55

"Bursting" Blueberry Maple Syrup Soft Serve Ice Cream	56
Peaches And Cream Soft Serve Ice Cream	57
Tropical Mango Soft Serve Ice Cream	58
Grapelicious Ice Cream	59
Astounding Apricot Almond Ice Cream	60
Kickin' Kiwi Lime Ice Cream	61
Vanilla Apple Cinnamon Ice Cream	62
Bursting Banana Nut Gelato	63
Apricot Honey Gelato	64
Big Blueberry Chocolate Gelato	65
Double Bliss Berry Delight Frozen Yogurt	66
Pulsating Pomegranate Mint Frozen Yogurt	67
Juicy Strawberry Honey Frozen Yogurt	68
Lemon Lime Milkshake	69
Double Cherry Chocolate Milkshake	70
Going Guava Milkshake	71
Caribbean Pineapple Sorbet	72
Mango Madness Coconut Raspberry Sorbet	73
Kickin' Key Lime Sorbet	74
Chunky Cherry Sorbet	75
Sassy Strawberry Lime Sorbet	76

Something Different — 77

Big Banana Nutella Soft Serve Ice Cream	78
Chocolate Peanut Butter Soft Serve Ice Cream	79
Basil Soft Serve Ice Cream	80
"Stuffed" Snickers Soft Serve Ice Cream	81
Matcha Ice Cream	82
Orange Dream Soda Ice Cream	83
Aromatic Earl Grey Tea Ice Cream	84
"Crispy' Kit Kat Ice Cream	85
Chocolaty Chocolate Pretzel Gelato	86
Chocolate Matcha Gelato	87
Aromatic Rose Gelato	88
Creamy White Chocolate Rose Frozen Yogurt	89
Chocolate Olive Oil Frozen Yogurt	90
Sweet Pumpkin Gingerbread Frozen Yogurt	91
Finger Lickin' Honey Lavender Milkshake	92

Fun Fig Mint Milkshake	93
Mouth Watering Maple Bacon Milkshake	94
Plum Sorbet	95
Clementine Sorbet	96
Luscious Lavender Sour Cherry Sorbet	97
Mango Madness Chili Lime Sorbet	98
Lingering Lemon Mint Sorbet	99

On The Healthy Side — 100

Vegan Chocolate Soft Serve Ice Cream	101
Vegan Radical Raspberry Chocolate Soft Serve Ice Cream	102
Vegan "Oh So" Soy Vanilla Soft Serve Ice Cream	103
Vegan Chunky Chocolate Almond Ice Cream	104
Vegan Sensuous Strawberries N Cream Ice Cream	105
Vegan Soy Vanilla And Carob Chip Ice Cream	106
Vegan Pistachio "Punch" Chocolate Chunk Gelato	107
Vegan Sweet Chocolate Strawberry Chunk Gelato	108
Vegan Big Blackberry Soy Frozen Yogurt	109
Vegan Ridiculous Raspberry Coconut Frozen Yogurt	110
Vegan Chunky Chocolate Banana Milkshake	111
Vegan Chocolate Made Mint Milkshake	112
Wonderful Watermelon Sorbet	113
Deep Dark Chocolate Sorbet	114

Child's Play — 115

Kiddo's Coca Cola Soft Serve Ice Cream	116
Double Bubble Gum Soft Serve Ice Cream	117
"Cool" Cake Batter Soft Serve Ice Cream	118
Caramel Corn Soft Serve Ice Cream	119
My Delicious M&M Ice Cream	120
Screamin' Sour Patch Kids Ice Cream	121
Dr. Pepper Ice Cream	122
Radical Root Beer Gelato	123
Three Musketeer Gelato	124
Crunchy Cinnamon Butterfinger Gelato	125
"Give Me More" S'mores Frozen Yogurt	126
Chilled Cherry Soda Frozen Yogurt	127
Cookies 'N Cream Rice Crispy Treat Frozen Yogurt	128
Red Velvet Milkshake	129

Peanut Butter Cup Milkshake	130
Crazy Cotton Candy Milkshake	131
Island Coconut Banana Sorbet	132

🍦 Grown Ups Only! — **133**
Double Gin And Tonic Soft Serve Ice Cream	134
Margarita Madness Soft Serve Ice Cream	136
Vanilla Screwdriver Soft Serve Ice Cream	136
"Adults Old Fashioned" Ice Cream	137
"New York" Manhattan Ice Cream	138
Creamy Kahlua Almond Delight Ice Cream	139
"Tasty" Tequila Sunrise Gelato	140
Runnin' Rum And Coke Gelato	141
Tropical Piña Colada Frozen Yogurt	142
Lickin' Lime Daiquiri Frozen Yogurt	143
The Guinness Chocolate Milkshake	144
Sunrise Strawberry Daiquiri Milkshake	145
Honey Cucumber Basil Rum Sorbet	146

🍦 Did You Appreciate This Publication? Here's What You Do Now... — **147**

🍦 A Little About The Author — **148**

🍦 Want Free Books? ... Of Course You Do! — **149**
Our New Books Sent To Your Email Monthly	149
Other Books We Highly Recommend!	150

Samantha Kaine

Our Complete Hamilton Beach® Ice Cream Recipe Book

Accessorizing Your Ice Cream

Start With A Base For Your Ice Cream

This easiest thing to do is to stick your ice cream in a bowl, and serve it. There are so many more tasty ways to serve your ice cream. Have some fun and let your imagination run wild. Here are some great choices to serve your ice cream like a pro.

- ✦ Waffle cone or cup
- ✦ Sugar cone
- ✦ Pretzel cone
- ✦ On pancakes or crepes
- ✦ On waffles
- ✦ On pie
- ✦ On cake
- ✦ On donuts
- ✦ On brownies
- ✦ In cookie cups
- ✦ In a chocolate dipped tortilla
- ✦ In between two cookies
- ✦ In a pie crust bowl
- ✦ In a cream puff
- ✦ On top of a grilled peach
- ✦ In between 2 pieces of pound cake

Toppings

This is where you can really go wild and have some fun. There's literally endless possibilities here. Any snack you enjoy will probably go with some type of ice cream. Fresh fruit is always a good healthy choice. Here are some choices to spark your imagination.

- Pretzel sticks
- Chocolate covered pretzels
- Breakfast cereal
- Brownies
- Marshmallows
- Chex mix
- Trail mix
- Sprinkles
- Graham crackers
- Sesame seeds
- Ritz crackers
- Chopped up candy bars
- Crushed lollipops
- Mochi
- Nuts
- M&M's
- Jelly beans
- Popcorn
- Cookies
- Gummy bears

- Dried fruit
- Whipped cream
- Chocolate chips
- Cocoa powder
- Cinnamon
- Vanilla
- Blueberries
- Raspberries
- Strawberries
- Apples
- Raisins
- Cherries
- Cranberries
- Bananas
- Currants
- Melon
- Peaches
- Pears
- Oranges
- Mango
- Pineapple

Don't Forget The Sauce

Sauces add lovely texture and flavor all at once. Sauce doesn't have to go on top however. Use sauces to decorate the plate or bowl. You can make your own sauces and put them in squeeze bottles to create beautiful designs. If you don't have time to make your own, your local grocery store carries many. Here are some sauces that compliment ice cream.

- Chocolate
- White chocolate
- Vanilla
- Butterscotch
- Caramel

- Blueberry
- Strawberry
- Raspberry
- Lemon
- Cherry
- Mocha

- Peanut butter
- Coffee
- Maple syrup
- Praline sauce
- Mint

Samantha Kaine

Chapter 1:
Why This Book Is A Must!

The Only Ice Cream Maker Book
For All Your Indulgences!

What dessert has been craved by kids and adults for all of eternity? That may be an over-exaggeration, but it's ice cream! The frozen treat has delighted so many for so long and now you have the ability to make delicious creations with the Hamilton Beach 4 Quart Ice Cream Maker!

Hamilton Beach has been a household name for decades; their products are incredibly durable and will last any cook a lifetime. They also are incredibly easy to use which allows you to make whatever you want without the stress; and who honestly wants stress while making ice cream? I guess if the reward eases the tension then it would make sense, but Hamilton Beach wants nothing to do with making things difficult.

The Hamilton Beach 4 Quart Ice Cream Maker will bring so much versatility to the kitchen that all sweet teeth will be satisfied after dinner. It's the only ice cream maker you need because it covers so many bases and palettes and is easy enough to use for anyone!

Sculpt Your Scoops!
The Art Of Frozen Yogurt, Ice Cream, & Sorbet

There's just something about making your own ice cream that sounds incredibly improbable. It's not like you have to drive out to the farm, tend to the cows, and do whatever it is farmers to do provide the public with delicious treats. With the Hamilton Beach 4 Quart Ice Cream Maker you don't need to worry about anything!

Now you get to stay home, avoid any unappetizing smells the farm has to offer, and get to making various ice cream creations. It's a different kind of skill. Bakers have baking and you creamers have creaming. Keep your mind on the dessert; we obvious aren't going to rephrase that. Ice cream making can turn from a quick-learning hobby into an expertise in no time with your new and reliable ice cream maker!

People are surprised when they are offered homemade ice cream. The astonishment of fresh and frozen treats leads to praise because it's a seemingly unachievable feat for an amateur in their eyes. Accept the acknowledgement now and thank the Hamilton Beach 4 Quart Ice Cream Maker later!

Samantha Kaine

31 Flavors??? Try 99!

The days of a small variety of flavors or watching a teenager mix together sugary ingredients on an expensive cold slab are over. Save your money and stay in! The only downfall with making your own ice cream is that you may end up spoiling everyone though.

Ice cream is for families to bond over, friends to share, couples to sinfully enjoy, and feelings to be mended alone. Imagine being able to have an assortment at your disposal at any time! The Hamilton Beach 4 Quart Ice Cream Maker gives you that option, making every warm summer night an ice cream night.

On the other hand, why limit yourself to the hotter months? Ice cream can be enjoyed during any season! You have the ability to pick the perfect dessert for the occasion. Just one example is Pumpkin Pie Ice Cream, the perfect treat for Halloween through Thanksgiving! Though that sounds complicated, it's very easy, and there are many more options just like it that can be made in no time at any time!

Master The Craft!

On second thought, who cares if you end up spoiling everyone. Is anyone really going to be complaining about being offered ice cream whenever they come over to your place? They deserve it, but more importantly, you deserve it! The Hamilton Beach 4 Quart Ice Cream Maker gives you the confidence to master your new favorite craft!

You will be able to feed the indulgences of every sweet tooth present, but make sure you take care of the cook as well. It's just not all the ice cream maker; your creative mind deserves praise also! You can learn new techniques, new collaborations, and new likes that could become the latest guilty pleasure.

So why wouldn't you want to spend time perfecting ice cream making? How *bad* can a bad experiment really be? It's ice cream so even the failed attempts will still be semi-delightful. Just watch out for anything crazy like meat (unless it's bacon of course) or eggplant or something. We're not trying to drive people away. You want people to come to your place and eat your ice cream!

The Possibilities Are Endless!

What's In This Ice Cream, you might ask...Anything you want! Anything that is edible actually, and an allergy check is also recommended before diving into the ingredient pool; we can't be giving people too much freedom. However, as already stressed, the possibilities are almost endless. You don't even have to stick to just ice cream; or, if you're a tad on the wild side, you don't even have to stick to one flavor in the same bowl!

Does someone not like chocolate (we don't know who, but they're out there)? No problem! Vanilla it is. Does someone not like either (now we're talking crazy)? Then strawberry or another fruit. Everyone can be as picky as they want because you're going to be able to find something they like. The Hamilton Beach 4 Quart Ice Cream Maker has you covered, even for those bacon lovers.

So go ahead and challenge yourself, challenge others even. No matter the occasion, no matter the special someone, no matter the flavor, your Hamilton Beach 4 Quart Ice Cream Maker will open up a new world of oh-so-good guilt!

Chapter 2:

This Ice Cream Maker Will Change The Life Of Your Dessert World!

The Dessert That Goes With Everything!

Have you ever been stuck in the unfortunate position of indecisiveness? Of course, in this context we're talking about what should we all have for dessert. Everyone doesn't seem to have an opinion other than they would definitely eat what is provided. Or worse, have you ever not had anything to offer? Good graces, how awful!

It's safe to say that ice cream goes with everything. However, because the Hamilton Beach 4 Quart Ice Cream Maker is so easy to use you can play the role of savior by saying, "Hey, I know what will go good with this meal. Ice cream!" Your guests will cheer and you will be the hero. Now get to work.
This book will also help you discover pairings you never thought possible. Who would have thought that ice cream can be so gourmet? Hamburgers, pasta, whatever you're having has a frozen dessert that will be perfect to finish with. Just having a sandwich? How about an ice cream sandwich to follow? We have come a long way since the basics; we need to use the progression of sweets!

The Old 31 Flavors Is A Thing of the Past...

No one likes to be limited or censored, that's a given. Of course chains don't have the resources to offer you endless flavors and creations, but we appreciate what they have done for the world of ice cream. We're gracious of their work for they have supported us through wonderful and hard times (break-ups primarily).

With that being said, you don't want to put them out of business, but then again, but you're free to do as you please at home. The Hamilton Beach 4 Quart Ice Cream Maker allows you do expand your horizons and be as bad as you want! Would people rather be stuck in an ice cream shop or free to say and enjoy whatever they want? Just remember, ice cream isn't just for kids. Silly rabbit. Or Silly cow more like it.

It's starting to become obvious, you have plenty of options and things to offer your family, friends, significant others, first dates, whoever when it comes to ice cream. Just sit back, relax, and enjoy the sweetest of sweets!

What's Not To Enjoy About Ice Cream?

Nothing. That was an easy question. There are so many flavors, so much sweetness that it makes being bad feel good! Desserts certainly get a bad rap from health nuts, but hey, just put some nuts in what you prepare for the naysayers and they will soon be right on board. You can even add some kale to appease the masses, but if that were the case, I personally would just accept the judgment instead of changing my dessert values.

The process of making ice cream is equally as enjoyable, and that's why choosing the Hamilton Beach 4 Quart Ice Cream Maker is an excellent decision. It just makes everything so much easier from adding the ingredients, letting the accessory do its thing, and then to the cleanup. Cooking, baking, and creaming all are very therapeutic, especially if you have the right equipment.

So you enjoy the taste, you enjoy the craft, and now you just have to enjoy the satisfaction. You've created something that brings smiles to the faces of others and gives you a sense of accomplishment. What more can you ask for? Again, nothing.

Strong As An Igloo!

This ice cream maker is extra strong and durable. We've come a long way since the first old school ice cream in the 40's and 50's but I tell you, in this book we bring that flavor right back! It's a timeless treat, and the Hamilton Beach 4 Quart Ice Cream Maker is made to withstand for generations.

The kitchen accessory is incredibly durable which is amazingly beneficial because you're going to want to use it over and over again. The ice cream maker is made of a stainless steel body and a double-insulated freezer bowl made to withstand the coldest of freezers. The heavy-duty motor is also a plus because it allows multiple uses, each being as easy as the first.

We can't stress enough that Hamilton Beach has been a staple in kitchens for decades and a trusted brand for generations. The next time your parents pass you down a small kitchen appliance, it's probably made by Hamilton Beach. That's great engineering and quality manufacturing if you ask me.

Safe, Sensible, & Smart!

The Hamilton Beach 4 Quart Ice Cream Maker is safe to use. Unlike the blades of a food processer, the accessory is easy to handle and assembly which allows you to even involve your children in the process. Also, there is a safety feature that will automatically shut off the maker if the motor is over-heating. This primarily happens if there are large and hard ingredients such as nuts or if the paddle has been excessively overused.

The small appliance is small enough to store away, and its form can fit anywhere in the kitchen. Also, if you decide to leave it out on the counter with your other impressive appliances then it will fit right in due to its stylish appearance. Sleek silver just promotes frozen delicacies!

As every Hamilton Beach product, the ice cream maker is incredibly smart, and the technology will last for generations. I mentioned the food processer earlier, and I'm going to be honest with you about it. My mother passed that down to me and I think it looks exactly the same as it did nearly four decades ago! You can't ask for a better brand, and the Hamilton Beach 4 Quart Ice Cream Maker is a great product.

Chapter 3:

Benefits Of This Frozen Yogurt, Sorbet And Ice Cream Maker!

Make Any Flavored Ice Cream You Want!

As long as there are ingredients sold where you shop then you can have any ice cream you desires, and given you probably use a grocery store or market then it's safe to say you're safe. This book provides you with a variety of recipes, but the beauty of ice cream is that you can be creative! Think about what you like the best; maybe chocolate, maybe cherries. Then put them together for a frozen treat!

I don't want to be the one to say it, but I will be: competition is apparent, especially with dessert. Everyone asks, "What's for dessert?" You can take the easy route and get something store-bought or you can impress with your own creation! Outdo your mother or mother-in-law with your own homemade style. Though their baked goods are irresistible, they have nothing on your ice cream!

When you impress you receive praise and respect, but what of the greatest forms of flattery is if someone asks for the recipe! And if you're nice then you will gladly share it. If you're even nicer then you will even say you used your Hamilton Beach 4 Quart Ice Cream Maker.

We've Got More Colors Than Crayola!

Flavors are one thing, but what about appearance? We're not talking about restaurants that overcharge for small portions of food just because they look nice. I mean, you still want to eat it instead of put it in a shadow box and on display forever. Fruit has different colors, as do flavorings, so go ahead and be colorful and creative! Make sure you take a picture because it won't last long.

Sweets are a delicate subject because if available they will be consumed; especially if you make them look incredibly appetizing. For example, if you have a strawberry and vanilla swirl with some black cherries mixed in and a mint leaf as garnish then it's going to attract indulgent eyes as if they were looking at a beautiful woman. Beauty and taste: a sinful combination.

So take your creamy, tasty, flavorful creation you made with your Hamilton Beach 4 Quart Ice Cream Maker, and enjoy with the ones who appreciate it the most: everyone. A perfect match every time.

The Best Of The Best!

The benefits that the Hamilton Beach 4 Quart Ice Cream Maker are easily shown in the end product, however, the process is what is truly magical. Hamilton Beach uses basic technology that has been proven to be the best on the market for many years.

The freezer bowl is perfectly-insulated to keep the ice cream cold, the paddle moves at your ideal speed to mix your ingredients evenly, and the lid is secure with an open spout for pouring, and easily removable when done so no one has to wait too long for their tasty treat! Hamilton Beach's warranty also proves they back their products, almost challenging you to find an issue. Spoiler alert: you won't.

Easy to setup and easy to use. The small appliance certainly is worth every penny and does most of the work for you. You just have to be creative! That shouldn't be too hard with all the recipes provided and the vast amount of creamy concoctions that await your touch!

BRRR! WAIT. THAT'S A GOOD THING!
Ice cream is cold. Duh. That means it needs to stay cold or it just becomes flavored milk. Super duh. The Hamilton Beach 4 Quart Ice Cream Maker does exactly that! No, it doesn't melt; it keeps it cold!

The double-insulated wall makes things cold fast and keeps them cold longer. However, the outside isn't as freezing so if you touch it you won't need to go to the doctor for frostbite. On a side note, don't lick the bowl, that will be embarrassing if you got stuck.

An important note before using: you must freeze the freezer bowl 6-22 hours prior to using it. It is recommended to use plastic wrap before freezing the bowl in order to prevent freezer burn. The back part of your freezer is where the temperature drops the most, so place it back there and the wait will soon be over!

Cleaning Is Just As Easy!

Though the Hamilton Beach 4 Quart Ice Cream Maker is a wonderful device, there will be some cleanup involved. However, you're in luck, because it's very easy to make sure everything is clean and tidy after you're done with your master creation! Simplicity is always the best trait of a great product.

You don't need anything fancy or any specific cleaning products. You simply need soap, water, and a damp cloth. What you don't need is a dishwasher, in fact, you're not supposed to put any of the parts of the ice cream maker in the dishwasher so make sure you're clear of using it. I know it's designed to make life easier, but so is your ice cream maker so take care of it.

The storage plug, cover, dasher, canister, and bucket can be washed in warm water with dish soap as if you were hand-washing any dish or utensil. Simple. As for the motor a clean cloth and wipe away and ingredients that unfortunately missed the bowl while creaming. Simple.

Chapter 4:

There's More Than Ice Cream On The Menu!

What Else Is There to Make?

We all have friends and family members who happen to be picky or unfortunately has a food allergy. A prime example being someone who is lactose intolerant. Why would they be reading this book you may ask? I will answer your question with another: why would they be writing this book as well?

Because it's ice cream and there are ways around it like taking a pill! Not everyone is as open as some authors, but there are different ways to please everyone. With the Hamilton Beach 4 Quart Ice Cream Maker you can make everything from diary to non-diary with ease!

Simple substitutes like almond, coconut, or soy milk can do the trick, even just organic lactose free milk is available... even goat milk! Okay, let's not go that far, unless you're into goats then be our guest. The point is that no matter the tongue, no matter the allergy, there is something for everyone; even people who don't like sweets that much can be happy! Just tone down the ingredients and you will be good. Freedom while making ice cream!

Samantha Kaine

Look Beyond The Cone...

What if that curmudgeon is just being too stubborn and refuses to eat ice cream? Then it's obvious: you don't invite them over ever again. However, that would be mean, and if they're a family member who resides in the house it would just be awkward. Simple solution: make something else with your Hamilton Beach 4 Quart Ice Cream Maker!

For the health nuts make some frozen yogurt; for the rich folk (taste not financial) you can easily stir up some gelato; for the tart and fruit lovers sorbet will do the trick; and for the people who prefer straws then you can concoct drinks even! Smoothies, slushes, whatever they fancy!

It's even used for parties... not a child's birthday bash, but when the kids are in beds or you're just having a slumber party for adults. Okay, we're talking about alcohol here if you didn't pick up on it. For example, margaritas and daiquiris can easily be mixed with you Hamilton Beach 4 Quart Ice Cream Maker. All you have to do is enjoy!

Make It Sinfully Delicious!

We touched on the basics, but don't forget the "I shouldn't" additions. Frozen yogurt chains have popularized the topping bar while you're out, offering tempting pleasures and taking advantage of the guiltiest of minds. Hey, you don't have to be ashamed; we know why you're there in the first place. On the other hand, why don't you mix it up at home!

Everything in the topping bar can be picked up at a grocery stores, probably even a convenient store at that. We know, we know, easy accessibility leads to other problems, but maybe if everyone had a little more ice cream then they can relax a little. Sometimes it's all right to spoil yourself!

Using your Hamilton Beach 4 Quart Ice Cream Maker, you can put any topping you like on your ice cream. Candy bars, sprinkles, nuts, fruit, mint leaves; and don't forget the syrups like fudge, caramel, and butterscotch. See, what's the problem with all that? Nothing!

I Scream, You Scream, We All Scream For Ice Cream... And More!

That's right, there are even more options. You have a Hamilton Beach 4 Quart Ice Cream Maker now, why just stop at the basics and garnishes. Use the versatility of the small appliance and get creative!

You can dip cones, pretzels and other salty snacks, and fruit with your favorite syrups. You can even use the ice cream you made to place it atop waffles or pancakes or another dessert your rival sister-in-law brought over because hers was just too plain and you had to dress it up a little. Ahh, rivalry.

How about some vanilla ice cream mixed with pecans and caramel syrup over a warm piece of apple pie. What's more American than apple pie? Apple pie loaded with other forms of sweet goodness. Let the creativity flow!

Chapter 5:
How To Use Your Ice Cream Maker!
Easy As 1-2-3

All these ideas are now flowing, you're ready to open up your creative genius, and all you want to do is get started. There are people waiting! First, let's make sure you know how to use the Hamilton Beach 4 Quart Ice Cream Maker.

Your HamiltonBeach Ice Cream Maker Parts

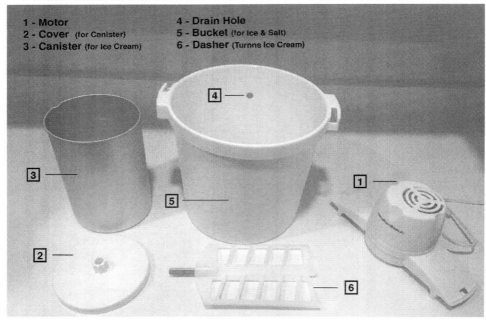

1 - Motor
2 - Cover (for Canister)
3 - Canister (for Ice Cream)
4 - Drain Hole
5 - Bucket (for Ice & Salt)
6 - Dasher (Turnns Ice Cream)

The Steps

1) Make sure your ice cream maker is clean and ready to use (even wash it before first use).

2) Prepare the ingredients in the recipes in a separate container beforehand. Make sure you can pour easily from your mixing container.

3) The bowl is designed to make no more than 4 quarts, and make sure not to fill the canister all the way to the top, fill it 2/3 full at most. The ingredients will increase the volume so be careful!

4) Pour the ingredients into the canister.

5) Secure the cover firmly onto the canister.

6) Put the canister in the middle of the bucket.

7) Put together the motor over canister. Make sure the dasher shaft is placed inside the hole in bottom of the motor. The motor is then counter clockwise to lock it in place on the bucket.

8) Plug the power cord in and allow the ingredients to churn for a minute or two.

9) Place 1 to 2 inches of ice in the bucket around the canister. Then cover with ½ cup of rock salt. Continue alternating until the canister has been covered.

10) Allow the ice cream to churn until the motor stops about 20-40 minutes, and transfer the concoction to another container, placing in the freezer for an additional 2 hours or more. Then enjoy!

There's More To It!

Learning about the Hamilton Beach 4 Quart Ice Cream Maker has really proved that ice cream making can be easy, fun, but even more surprising, amazingly versatile! It's not just the sweetness that is to be had or the guilty pleasures that are to be appeased, but the variety of ingredients offered.

While shopping you like to get a good mixture of what is quality and what you can afford. Sweet treats are easily attainable, and really do not break the bank. Not to mention, they are all over the place! Stores make it easy to buy what you need, and the Hamilton Beach 4 Quart Ice Cream Maker makes it easy to make your creations!

Though you don't want to break the bank, and you probably won't, make sure the fruit you pick, the toppings you choose, and the mixers you decide on are good brands. You don't want to disappoint! There are greats brands of milk out there, chocolate chips, candy bars, and syrups so use what your taste buds like the most. You have plenty of opportunities to experiment now..

Presentation Is Always a Must!

We have mentioned this before, but presentation can really liven up your ice cream. Your creations deserve attention because you are becoming a master and why not add a little pizazz to the mix. It will impress as much as the taste does!

Gourmet is starting to become a very popular style in all meals once again, and to dress something up such as ice cream is quite impressive. After using your Hamilton Beach 4 Quart Ice Cream Maker over and over you will have adopted a very quirky and fun skill that can bring joy to many people, so you may as well take it to the next level with garnishes.

Say you made some mint chocolate chip ice cream. Add some mint leaves, peppermint bark, and perhaps one full strawberry to the final product and you have yourself a gorgeous and mouth-watering treat! It's just too bad you have to eat it, but we know everyone can't resist.

Our Complete Hamilton Beach® Ice Cream Recipe Book

Chapter 6:
Things The Pros Know!

You Don't Have To Feel So Guilty!

Ice cream has never been confused for being healthy. On the other hand, fruit has! It's all about finding a medium so you don't have to feel so bad after feeling so good. The addition of fruits can make your tasteful delight even more attractive to a wider audience!

Fruit has natural sugars, pure sweet nectar that has been used for so many things over centuries. The old adage goes, "An apple a day keeps the doctor away." We're big advocates of being healthy so if you somehow miss eating your daily apple or other piece of fruit, then mix it in to your dessert just in case!

We're not saying eat a caramel apple and you're set, but the addition of berries, bananas, and oranges, amongst other fruits, will not only enhance your frozen treat, but bring a healthier aspect to the table. Therefore, you don't have to feel so guilty and you still get to use your Hamilton Beach 4 Quart Ice Cream Maker!

Be An Inventor... Create That Ice Cream Dream!

So you have your Hamilton Beach 4 Quart Ice Cream Maker, you have your ideas, and now you have your experience. What's next? How do you get that creativity out when you seemingly have plateaued with vanilla and chocolate variations?

You want to get to another level of ice cream making that transforms you from family celebrity to master creamer. There is no reason to stay in the same place when you can keep progressing; especially when you have a machine that allows you to do so.

The pros have certain techniques that can help you reach a certain level. Best advice: keep it cold! That is obvious, but even when your pouring ingredients and syrup into the mix, you don't want anything to really warm up too quickly. Preparation is just as important as the creativity! Be prepared, keep it cold, and use common pairings like dark chocolate and cherry as a base for other flavor combinations!

Chapter 7:
Storage For Later!

Captain Obvious Says, "Keep It Cold."

Yes, yes, yes. We didn't mean to be *mean*, but the truth must be stressed. Ice cream, frozen yogurt, sorbet, gelato, and frozen drinks all need to stay cold! When syrup melts it's just liquid sugar and really isn't that great. It's important to keep the flavors contained instead of dripping all over the place.

You made ice cream for a reason, you didn't make milk; you have milk, you didn't accomplish much by obtaining that milk, and you can have it whenever. Ice cream is cold and delicious and needs to stay that way, so keep it frozen!

It is recommended that your freezer be set at 0 degrees in order to store your frosty creations.

Channel Your Inner Tetris

There is an art to storing food, and it takes an organized mind. Refrigerators and freezers can become cluttered so you need to be aware of where to put what.

First you have to choose the right containers and storage bags. Air causes freezer burn so you want to make sure everything is tight, and if you're using bags, push all the air out before sealing. Also, make sure to label what your storing so you don't defrost the wrong thing! With that being said, it is wise to portion your leftovers because defrosting then refreezing isn't the best!

Make sure what you are putting in the freezer should be frozen and for later use; some foods may go bad no matter what. Lay everything flat because it makes things stackable and opens up to room to organize. Lastly, remember the temperature difference. The back is the coldest and the door is the warmest. Best advice: no ice cream in the door for risk of melting!

Destroy The Evidence!

We've mentioned ice cream can be messy, but we probably didn't need to say it twice. You can't even eat it out of a bowl without something dripping somewhere! So imagine what making ice cream would be like. It's not that bad because it's so easy with the Hamilton Beach 4 Quart Ice Cream Maker!

Because of its one bowl design, everything is contained, but there is also less to clean. We've talked about how to properly wash the parts and the base, but after you're done, where does it go? Just tuck it away: it's that simple!

Make sure everything is dry; they can rest tucked away in the cabinet or a corner of your counter. Perfect!

Satisfy The Sweet Tooth!

There no longer a reason to pay attention to the bell outside slowly annoying the neighborhood and there is no reason for a container to be in the freezer anymore. You have your Hamilton Beach 4 Quart Ice Cream Maker and now you're the master!

To recap: there are endless possibilities of creativity to make devilishly delicious treats, the Hamilton Beach 4 Quart Ice Cream Maker is so simple to use, and it will help you please everyone!

So surprise your family, impress a date with sinful temptation, or just spoil yourself and feed your guilty pleasures. Delicious ice cream awaits!

The Classics

All of the flavors you can imagine are in this delicious ice cream book, however, you can never escape the classics. Your good old favorite classic ice creams are here for the indulging! Enjoy!

Classic Vanilla Soft-Serve Ice Cream

Nothing says comfort like vanilla ice cream. It's the classic taste you grew up with. This ice cream is simply made with 4 ingredients, and is oh so delicious.

Prep Time: 35 Minutes
Servings: 6

INGREDIENTS
2 cups heavy cream
1 cup milk
¾ cup sugar
1 Tbs. vanilla extract

DIRECTIONS

- Place the milk and cream in a bowl, and mix them together until well combined. Use a whisk to mix in the sugar. Continue to whisk for about 4 minutes until the sugar dissolves. Then mix in the vanilla extract.

- Pour the ingredients into the canister, follow the instructions above to set up your ice cream maker, and let it churn for 25 minutes.

- Serve immediately.

Chunky Chocolate Chip Soft Serve Ice Cream

The chocolate chips give a rich flavor to the delicate vanilla ice cream. Try using dark chocolate chips if you want a real contrast in flavors.

Prep Time: 35 Minutes
Servings: 6

INGREDIENTS
2 cups heavy cream
1 cup milk
¾ cup sugar
1 Tbs. vanilla extract
1 cup chocolate chips of your choice

DIRECTIONS
- Place the milk and cream in a bowl, and mix them together until well combined. Use a whisk to mix in the sugar. Continue to whisk for about 4 minutes until the sugar dissolves. Then mix in the vanilla extract.

- Pour all the ingredients into the canister and stir well, follow the instructions above to set up your ice cream maker, and let it churn for 25 minutes.

- Serve immediately.

California Cookies-N-Cream Soft Serve Ice Cream

This all-time classic combines the delicious flavors of vanilla ice cream and chocolate sandwich cookies. The rich taste of the sandwich cookies is complimented by the subtle creaminess of the vanilla ice cream.

Prep Time: 35 Minutes
Servings: 6

INGREDIENTS
  2 cups heavy cream
  1 cup milk
  ¾ cup sugar
  1 Tbs. vanilla extract
  20 chocolate sandwich cookies

DIRECTIONS

✦ Place the milk and cream in a bowl, and mix them together until well combined. Use a whisk to mix in the sugar. Continue to whisk for about 4 minutes until the sugar dissolves. Then mix in the vanilla extract.

✦ Place the sandwich cookies in a food processor, and process until the cookies are no bigger than chocolate chips. If you don't have a food processor place the cookies in a large resealable plastic bag, and seal it shut. Use your hands, a mallet, or a rolling pin to crush the cookies.

✦ Pour all the ingredients into the canister and stir well, follow the instructions above to set up your ice cream maker, and let it churn for 25 minutes.

✦ Serve immediately.

Radical Rocky Road Ice Cream

This ice cream is filled with different textures thanks to the soft marshmallows, and hard nuts. The flavors combine with the chocolate to create a sweet, rich, delicious ice cream.

Prep Time: 2 Hours 50 Minutes
Servings: 6

INGREDIENTS
- 2 cups heavy cream
- 1 cup milk
- 3/4 cup sugar
- 1 Tbs. vanilla extract
- ½ cup unsweetened cocoa powder
- ½ cup chopped pecans
- 1 cup mini marshmallows

DIRECTIONS
✦ Place the milk and cream in a bowl, and mix them together until well combined. Use a whisk to mix in the sugar. Continue to whisk for about 4 minutes until the sugar dissolves. Then whisk in cocoa powder until all lumps are gone, and well mixed. Then mix in the vanilla extract.

✦ Pour all the ingredients into the canister and stir well, follow the instructions above to set up your ice cream maker, and let it churn for 25 minutes.

✦ Put the ice cream in an airtight container and place in the freezer for around 2 hours. Allow the ice cream to thaw for 15 minutes before serving.

Miraculous Double Mint Chip Ice Cream

This classic ice cream is comfort in a bowl. The fresh, sweet, aromatic taste of the mint it complimented by the strong flavor of the chocolate.

Prep Time: 2 Hours 50 Minutes
Servings: 6

INGREDIENTS
   2 cups heavy cream
   1 cup milk
   3/4 cup sugar
   1 teaspoon vanilla extract
   1 teaspoon peppermint extract
   1 cup semi-sweet chocolate chips

DIRECTIONS
- Place the milk and cream in a bowl, and mix them together until well combined. Use a whisk to mix in the sugar. Continue to whisk for about 4 minutes until the sugar dissolves. Then mix in the vanilla and peppermint extract.

- Pour all the ingredients into the canister and stir well, follow the instructions above to set up your ice cream maker, and let it churn for 25 minutes.

- Put the ice cream in an airtight container and place in the freezer for around 2 hours. Allow the ice cream to thaw for 15 minutes before serving.

Power Punch Pistachio Ice Cream

This flavor is one of the 3 parts of spumoni ice cream. It has a light nutty flavor that's light, and creamy.

Prep Time: 2 Hours 50 Minutes
Servings: 6

INGREDIENTS
- 2 cups heavy cream
- 1 cup milk
- 3/4 cup sugar
- 1/4 teaspoon almond extract
- 1/2 cup chopped pistachios

DIRECTIONS
- Place the milk and cream in a bowl, and mix them together until well combined. Use a whisk to mix in the sugar. Continue to whisk for about 4 minutes until the sugar dissolves. Then mix in the almond extract.

- Pour all the ingredients into the canister and stir well, follow the instructions above to set up your ice cream maker, and let it churn for 25 minutes.

- Put the ice cream in an airtight container and place in the freezer for around 2 hours. Allow the ice cream to thaw for 15 minutes before serving.

Double Dark Chocolate Gelato

This classic has all the chocolaty flavor you can handle. It has a dense chocolate flavor that chocoholics will crave!

Prep Time: 2 Hours 35 Minutes
Servings: 4-6

INGREDIENTS

- 1/2 cup heavy cream
- 2 cups milk
- 3/4 cup sugar
- 1/4 teaspoon salt
- 7 ounces high quality dark chocolate
- 1 teaspoon vanilla extract

DIRECTIONS

- Melt the chocolate, and allow it to cool a little bit.

- Place the milk and cream in a bowl, and mix them together until well combined. Use a whisk to mix in the sugar and salt. Continue to whisk for about 4 minutes until the sugar and salt dissolve. Then mix in the vanilla extract. Finally mix in the chocolate until well combined.

- Pour the ingredients into the canister, follow the instructions above to set up your ice cream maker, and let it churn for 25 minutes.

- Put the gelato in an airtight container and place in the freezer for up to 2 hours, until desired consistency is reached.

Very Strawberry Gelato

This gelato has an intense strawberry flavor. It goes really well with a nice piece of chocolate cake.

Prep Time: 2 Hours 35 Minutes
Servings: 4-6

INGREDIENTS
- 1/2 cup heavy cream
- 2 cups milk
- 3/4 cup sugar
- 1 cup sliced strawberries
- 1 tablespoon vanilla extract

DIRECTIONS
- ✦ Puree the strawberries in a food processor or blender.
- ✦ Place the milk and cream in a bowl, and mix them together until well combined. Use a whisk to mix in the sugar. Continue to whisk for about 4 minutes until the sugar dissolves. Then mix in the vanilla extract and strawberry puree.
- ✦ Pour the ingredients into the canister, follow the instructions above to set up your ice cream maker, and let it churn for 25 minutes.
- ✦ Put the gelato in an airtight container and place in the freezer for up to 2 hours, until desired consistency is reached.

Chocolate Chip Cookie Dough Frozen Yogurt

This yogurt has a creamy vanilla base that allows the cookie dough to shine. The sweet flavors of cookie dough and chocolate take center stage in this classic.

Prep Time: 2 Hours 35 Minutes
Servings: 1 Quart

INGREDIENTS
- *1 quart container full-fat plain yogurt*
- *¼ teaspoon salt*
- *1 cup sugar*
- *1 tablespoon vanilla extract*
- *½ cup prepackaged cookie dough cut into small chunks*

DIRECTIONS

✦ Place the yogurt in a bowl. Use a whisk to mix in the sugar and salt. Continue to whisk for about 4 minutes until the sugar dissolves. Then mix in the vanilla extract.

✦ Pour all the ingredients into the canister and stir well, follow the instructions above to set up your ice cream maker, and let it churn for 25 minutes.

✦ Put the frozen yogurt in an airtight container and place in the freezer for at least 2 hours, until desired consistency is reached.

Divine Coffee Frozen Yogurt

This makes a great pick me up on a hot summer day instead of regular coffee. Use decaf coffee if you don't want a buzz.

Prep Time: 2 Hours 35 Minutes
Servings: 1 Quart

INGREDIENTS
1 quart container full-fat plain yogurt
¼ teaspoon salt
1 cup sugar
1 teaspoon vanilla extract
1 cup strong brewed coffee or espresso
1 tablespoon coffee grounds

DIRECTIONS

✦ Place the yogurt in a bowl. Use a whisk to mix in the sugar and salt. Continue to whisk for about 4 minutes until the sugar dissolves. Then mix in the vanilla extract, coffee, and coffee grounds.

✦ Pour the ingredients into the canister, follow the instructions above to set up your ice cream maker, and let it churn for 25 minutes.

✦ Put the frozen yogurt in an airtight container and place in the freezer for at least 2 hours, until desired consistency is reached.

Pralines And "Oh So Creamy" Milkshake

This classic milkshake combines creamy ice cream with rich buttery pecans. Make sure you chop your pecans small enough to fit through a straw.

Prep Time: 25 Minutes
Servings: 6

INGREDIENTS

- 2 cups heavy cream
- 1 cup milk
- 1 cup brown sugar
- 1 teaspoon vanilla extract
- 1/3 cup finely chopped pecans
- 1 tablespoon butter

DIRECTIONS

✦ Melt the butter in a small skillet on medium heat. Add the pecans, and cook for about 5 minutes, until they become lightly browned.

✦ Place the milk and cream in a bowl, and mix them together until well combined. Use a whisk to mix in the sugar. Continue to whisk for about 4 minutes until the sugar dissolves. Then mix in the vanilla extract.

✦ Pour all the ingredients into the canister and stir well, follow the instructions above to set up your ice cream maker, and let it churn for 10-15 minutes, until desired consistency is reached.

✦ Serve immediately.

Mint Cookies 'N Cream "Silkshake"

This a twist of two classic ice cream flavors. You get the mint and chocolate flavor of mint chip with the cookie texture of cookies 'n cream.

Prep Time: 25 Minutes
Servings: 6

INGREDIENTS
- 2 cups heavy cream
- 1 cup milk
- 3/4 cup sugar
- 1 teaspoon vanilla extract
- 1 ½ teaspoons mint extract
- 10 chocolate sandwich cookies

DIRECTIONS
- Place the milk and cream in a bowl, and mix them together until well combined. Use a whisk to mix in the sugar. Continue to whisk for about 4 minutes until the sugar dissolves. Then mix in the vanilla and mint extract.

- Place the sandwich cookies in a food processor, and process until the cookies are no bigger than chocolate chips. If you don't have a food processor place the cookies in a large resealable plastic bag, and seal it shut. Use your hands, a mallet, or a rolling pin to crush the cookies.

- Pour all the ingredients into the canister and stir well, follow the instructions above to set up your ice cream maker, and let it churn for 10-15 minutes, until desired consistency is reached.

- Serve immediately.

Fruitilicious

In this section we show you how fruit has never tasted this good! When you mix fruit flavors with your favorite ice cream you get something that is incredibly "FRUITILICIOUS!!"

"Bursting" Blueberry Maple Syrup Soft Serve Ice Cream

This ice cream tastes like blueberry pancakes. It has a beautiful purple color, and is a perfect summer ice cream recipes.

Prep Time: 35 Minutes
Servings: 6

INGREDIENTS
- 2 cups heavy cream
- 1 cup milk
- ¾ cup sugar
- 1 Tbs. vanilla extract
- 1 cup blueberries
- ¼ cup maple syrup

DIRECTIONS

- Puree the blueberries in a food processor or blender.

- Place the milk and cream in a bowl, and mix them together until well combined. Use a whisk to mix in the sugar. Continue to whisk for about 4 minutes until the sugar dissolves. Then mix in the vanilla extract. Then mix in the blueberries, and maple syrup.

- Pour the ingredients into the canister, follow the instructions above to set up your ice cream maker, and let it churn for 25 minutes.

- Serve immediately.

Peaches and Cream Soft Serve Ice Cream

Here's an ice cold twist on this southern favorite. Making this dessert into ice cream accentuates the creaminess, and heightens the flavors. The flavor of the cream compliments the delicate flavor of the peaches.

Prep Time: 35 Minutes
Servings: 6

INGREDIENTS

2 cups heavy cream
1 cup milk
¾ cup sugar
1 Tbs. vanilla extract
1 cup sliced peaches

DIRECTIONS

✦ Puree the peaches in a food processor or blender.

✦ Place the milk and cream in a bowl, and mix them together until well combined. Use a whisk to mix in the sugar. Continue to whisk for about 4 minutes until the sugar dissolves. Then mix in the vanilla extract. Then mix in the peaches.

✦ Pour the ingredients into the canister, follow the instructions above to set up your ice cream maker, and let it churn for 25 minutes.

✦ Serve immediately.

Tropical Mango Soft Serve Ice Cream

There aren't many things that are more refreshing than a sweet, tropical mango. Mangos become even more refreshing in this delicious, creamy soft serve ice cream.

Prep Time: 35 Minutes
Servings: 6

INGREDIENTS
 2 cups heavy cream
 1 cup milk
 ¾ cup sugar
 1 Tbs. vanilla extract
 1 cup pureed mango (about 2.5 mangos)
 Juice of 1 lime

DIRECTIONS
✦ Puree the mangos with the lime juice in a food processor or blender.

✦ Place the milk and cream in a bowl, and mix them together until well combined. Use a whisk to mix in the sugar. Continue to whisk for about 4 minutes until the sugar dissolves. Then mix in the vanilla extract. Then mix in the mango puree.

✦ Pour the ingredients into the canister, follow the instructions above to set up your ice cream maker, and let it churn for 25 minutes.

✦ Serve immediately.

Grapelicious Ice Cream

This is one you probably haven't tried before. It has a deep grape flavor thanks to the grape juice concentrate. The concentrate is used instead of fresh grapes, because the skins destroy the texture of the ice cream, but contain most of the grape flavor.

Prep Time: 2 Hours 50 Minutes
Servings: 6

INGREDIENTS

2 cups heavy cream
1 cup milk
3/4 cup sugar
1 teaspoon vanilla extract
2 cans (12 ounces) frozen grape juice concentrate
juice of 3 lemons

DIRECTIONS

- Place the milk and cream in a bowl, and mix them together until well combined. Use a whisk to mix in the sugar. Continue to whisk for about 4 minutes until the sugar dissolves. Then mix in the vanilla extract, grape juice, and lemon juice.

- Pour the ingredients into the canister, follow the instructions above to set up your ice cream maker, and let it churn for 25 minutes.

- Put the ice cream in an airtight container and place in the freezer for around 2 hours. Allow the ice cream to thaw for 15 minutes before serving.

Astounding Apricot Almond Ice Cream

Apricots give this ice cream a delicious sweet, and fresh flavor. The almonds add a nice crunch, and a deep nutty flavor to compliment the apricots.

Prep Time: 2 Hours 50 Minutes
Servings: 6

INGREDIENTS
   2 cups heavy cream
   1 cup milk
   3/4 cup sugar
   1 teaspoon vanilla extract
   1 cup sliced apricots
   ½ cup chopped almonds

DIRECTIONS
✦ Puree the apricots in a food processor or blender.

✦ Place the milk and cream in a bowl, and mix them together until well combined. Use a whisk to mix in the sugar. Continue to whisk for about 4 minutes until the sugar dissolves. Then mix in the vanilla extract, and apricot puree.

✦ Pour all the ingredients into the canister and stir well, follow the instructions above to set up your ice cream maker, and let it churn for 25 minutes.

✦ Put the ice cream in an airtight container and place in the freezer for around 2 hours. Allow the ice cream to thaw for 15 minutes before serving.

Kickin' Kiwi Lime Ice Cream

This is a tropical ice cream that's perfect for summer. The kiwi gives the ice cream a light sweet flavor that's balanced by the tanginess of the lime. This ice cream has a subtle flavor.

Prep Time: 2 Hours 50 Minutes
Servings: 6

INGREDIENTS

- 2 cups heavy cream
- 1 cup milk
- 3/4 cup sugar
- 1/2 teaspoon vanilla extract
- ½ teaspoon salt
- 1 kiwi, peeled
- Juice of one and a half limes

DIRECTIONS

✦ Puree the kiwi in a food processor or blender.

✦ Place the milk and cream in a bowl, and mix them together until well combined. Use a whisk to mix in the sugar and salt. Continue to whisk for about 4 minutes until the sugar and salt dissolves. Then mix in the vanilla extract, lime juice, and kiwi puree.

✦ Pour the ingredients into the canister, follow the instructions above to set up your ice cream maker, and let it churn for 25 minutes.

✦ Put the ice cream in an airtight container and place in the freezer for around 2 hours. Allow the ice cream to thaw for 15 minutes before serving.

Vanilla Apple Cinnamon Ice Cream

This ice cream is reminiscent of apple pie, and is great for fall and winter. The cinnamon has a great warmth that heightens the flavor of the apples, and walnuts.

Prep Time: 2 Hours 50 Minutes
Servings: 6

INGREDIENTS

- 2 cups heavy cream
- 1 cup milk
- 3/4 cup sugar
- 1 teaspoon vanilla extract
- 1 teaspoon ground cinnamon
- 2 large apples peeled, cored, and sliced
- 1/4 cup chopped walnuts

DIRECTIONS

- Puree the apples in a food processor or blender.

- Place the milk and cream in a bowl, and mix them together until well combined. Use a whisk to mix in the sugar. Continue to whisk for about 4 minutes until the sugar dissolves. Then mix in the vanilla extract, cinnamon, and apple puree.

- Pour all the ingredients into the canister and stir well, follow the instructions above to set up your ice cream maker, and let it churn for 25 minutes.

- Put the ice cream in an airtight container and place in the freezer for around 2 hours. Allow the ice cream to thaw for 15 minutes before serving.

Bursting Banana Nut Gelato

This gelato has a full banana flavor that's not too sweet. The walnuts give the gelato crunchiness, and give it a nice richness.

Prep Time: 2 Hours 35 Minutes
Servings: 4-6

INGREDIENTS
1/2 cup heavy cream
2 cups milk
3/4 cup sugar
1 tablespoon vanilla extract
1 cup sliced banana
½ cup chopped walnuts

DIRECTIONS
+ Puree the bananas in a food processor or blender.

+ Place the milk and cream in a bowl, and mix them together until well combined. Use a whisk to mix in the sugar. Continue to whisk for about 4 minutes until the sugar dissolves. Then mix in the vanilla extract and banana puree.

+ Pour all the ingredients into the canister and stir well, follow the instructions above to set up your ice cream maker, and let it churn for 25 minutes.

+ Put the gelato in an airtight container and place in the freezer for up to 2 hours, until desired consistency is reached.

Apricot Honey Gelato

The apricot gives this gelato a sweet and tart flavor. The honey gives a light flavor that helps cut through the tartness of the apricot.

Prep Time: 2 Hours 35 Minutes
Servings: 4-6

INGREDIENTS
- 1/2 cup heavy cream
- 2 cups milk
- 3/4 cup sugar
- 1 tablespoon vanilla extract
- 1 cup sliced apricot
- 1/4 cup honey

DIRECTIONS
- Puree the apricots in a food processor or blender.

- Place the milk and cream in a bowl, and mix them together until well combined. Use a whisk to mix in the sugar. Continue to whisk for about 4 minutes until the sugar dissolves. Then mix in the vanilla extract honey and apricot puree.

- Pour the ingredients into the canister, follow the instructions above to set up your ice cream maker, and let it churn for 25 minutes.

- Put the gelato in an airtight container and place in the freezer for up to 2 hours, until desired consistency is reached.

Samantha Kaine

Big Blueberry Chocolate Gelato

This gelato has a great balance of rich and sweet flavors. The chocolate has a rich, complex flavor that's balanced by the sweetness of the blueberries.

Prep Time: 2 Hours 35 Minutes
Servings: 4-6

INGREDIENTS
- 1/2 cup heavy cream
- 2 cups milk
- 3/4 cup sugar
- 1 teaspoon vanilla extract
- 1 cup blueberries
- ½ cup finely chopped semi-sweet

DIRECTIONS
- ✦ Puree the bananas in a food processor or blender.

- ✦ Place the milk and cream in a bowl, and mix them together until well combined. Use a whisk to mix in the sugar. Continue to whisk for about 4 minutes until the sugar dissolves. Then mix in the vanilla extract and banana puree.

- ✦ Pour all the ingredients into the canister and stir well, follow the instructions above to set up your ice cream maker, and let it churn for 25 minutes.

- ✦ Put the gelato in an airtight container and place in the freezer for up to 2 hours, until desired consistency is reached.

Double Bliss Berry Delight Frozen Yogurt

This makes a great pick me up on a hot summer day instead of regular coffee. Use decaf coffee if you don't want a buzz.

Prep Time: 2 Hours 35 Minutes
Servings: 1 Quart

INGREDIENTS
1 quart container full-fat plain yogurt
¼ teaspoon salt
1 cup sugar
1 tablespoon vanilla extract
1 cup raspberries
1 cup blueberries

DIRECTIONS

✦ Puree the raspberries and blueberries in a food processor or blender

✦ Place the yogurt in a bowl. Use a whisk to mix in the sugar and salt. Continue to whisk for about 4 minutes until the sugar dissolves. Then mix in the vanilla extract, and berry puree.

✦ Pour the ingredients into the canister, follow the instructions above to set up your ice cream maker, and let it churn for 25 minutes.

✦ Put the frozen yogurt in an airtight container and place in the freezer for at least 2 hours, until desired consistency is reached.

Pulsating Pomegranate Mint Frozen Yogurt

This yogurt has full flavor thanks to the sweetness of the pomegranate, the freshness of the mint, and the richness of the chocolate. Use less mint extract if you want a more robust pomegranate flavor.

Prep Time: 2 Hours 35 Minutes
Servings: 1 Quart

INGREDIENTS
1 quart container full-fat plain yogurt
¼ teaspoon salt
1 cup sugar
1 tablespoon mint extract
1 cup 100% pomegranate juice
1/2 cup semi-sweet chocolate chips

DIRECTIONS

✦ Place the yogurt in a bowl. Use a whisk to mix in the sugar and salt. Continue to whisk for about 4 minutes until the sugar dissolves. Then mix in the mint extract, and pomegranate juice.

✦ Pour all the ingredients into the canister and stir well, follow the instructions above to set up your ice cream maker, and let it churn for 25 minutes.

✦ Put the frozen yogurt in an airtight container and place in the freezer for at least 2 hours, until desired consistency is reached.

Juicy Strawberry Honey Frozen Yogurt

Strawberries just scream summertime, and childhood for a lot of people. The strawberry flavor is enhanced by the sweet, rich taste of honey.

Prep Time: 2 Hours 35 Minutes
Servings: 1 Quart

INGREDIENTS
1 quart container full-fat plain yogurt
¼ teaspoon salt
1 cup sugar
1 teaspoon vanilla extract
8 ounces strawberries
1/4 cup honey

DIRECTIONS
✦ Puree the strawberries in a food processor or blender.

✦ Place the yogurt in a bowl. Use a whisk to mix in the sugar and salt. Continue to whisk for about 4 minutes until the sugar dissolves. Then mix in the vanilla extract, honey and strawberry puree.

✦ Pour the ingredients into the canister, follow the instructions above to set up your ice cream maker, and let it churn for 25 minutes.

✦ Put the frozen yogurt in an airtight container and place in the freezer for at least 2 hours, until desired consistency is reached.

Lemon Lime Milkshake

This is a natural version of sprite in milkshake form. The lemon and lime flavors are tangy and refreshing.

Prep Time: 25 Minutes
Servings: 6

INGREDIENTS
2 cups heavy cream
1 cup milk
3/4 cup sugar
1 teaspoon vanilla extract
¼ cup lime juice
¼ cup lemon juice
Zest of one lemon
Zest of one lime

DIRECTIONS
- Place the milk and cream in a bowl, and mix them together until well combined. Use a whisk to mix in the sugar. Continue to whisk for about 4 minutes until the sugar dissolves. Then mix in the vanilla extract, juice, and zest.

- Pour the ingredients into the canister, follow the instructions above to set up your ice cream maker, and let it churn for 10-15 minutes, until desired consistency is reached.

- Serve immediately.

Double Cherry Chocolate Milkshake

This is a natural version of sprite in milkshake form. The lemon and lime flavors are tangy and refreshing.

Prep Time: 25 Minutes
Servings: 6

INGREDIENTS
    2 cups heavy cream
    1 cup milk
    3/4 cup sugar
    1 teaspoon vanilla extract
    1 cup cherry juice
    ¼ cup semi-sweet chocolate chips

DIRECTIONS
- Place the milk and cream in a bowl, and mix them together until well combined. Use a whisk to mix in the sugar. Continue to whisk for about 4 minutes until the sugar dissolves. Then mix in the vanilla extract, and cherry juice.

- Pour all the ingredients into the canister and stir well, follow the instructions above to set up your ice cream maker, and let it churn for 10-15 minutes, until desired consistency is reached.

- Serve immediately.

Going Guava Milkshake

This is a natural version of sprite in milkshake form. The lemon and lime flavors are tangy and refreshing.

Prep Time: 25 Minutes
Servings: 6

INGREDIENTS
2 cups heavy cream
1 cup milk
3/4 cup sugar
1 teaspoon vanilla extract
1 1/2 cups guava juice

DIRECTIONS
- Place the milk and cream in a bowl, and mix them together until well combined. Use a whisk to mix in the sugar. Continue to whisk for about 4 minutes until the sugar dissolves. Then mix in the vanilla extract, and juice.

- Pour the ingredients into the canister, follow the instructions above to set up your ice cream maker, and let it churn for 10-15 minutes, until desired consistency is reached.

- Serve immediately.

Caribbean Pineapple Sorbet

This sorbet is perfect when you want to cool down on a hot day, the pineapple is incredibly refreshing. Try serving it for dessert after a fish dinner or teriyaki chicken.

Prep Time: 2 hours 40 Minutes
Servings: 9

INGREDIENTS
1 diced, peeled, and cored small pineapple
2 tablespoons lemon juice
1 cup plus 2 tablespoons sugar

DIRECTIONS
✦ Puree the pineapple and lemon juice in a food processor or blender. Then add in the sugar and puree until the sugar dissolves.

✦ Pour the ingredients into the canister, follow the instructions above to set up your ice cream maker, and let it churn for 25-30 minutes.

✦ Place in an airtight container for up to 2 hours, until desired consistency is reached.

Mango Madness Coconut Raspberry Sorbet

The mango and coconut give this sorbet a lovely creaminess. The raspberries give this tropical sorbet a nice tartness.

Prep Time: 5 hours 35 Minutes
Servings: 11

INGREDIENTS
3 cups packed, cubed mango
1 cup fresh raspberries
1 cup full-fat coconut milk
1 cup sugar
Pinch of salt
1 teaspoon lime juice

DIRECTIONS
- Puree all the ingredients in a food processor or blender. Then transfer the mixture to a bowl, and refrigerate covered for 3-4 hours.

- Pour the ingredients into the canister, follow the instructions above to set up your ice cream maker, and let it churn for 25-30 minutes.

- Place in an airtight container for up to 2 hours, until desired consistency is reached.

Kickin' Key Lime Sorbet

This has all the great flavor of key lime pie. This sorbet has a nice mix of sweet and tart.

Prep Time: 3 hours
Servings: 4

INGREDIENTS
  3 cups cold water
  2 ¼ cup fresh key lime juice
  2 3/4 cup sugar
  1 tablespoon lime zest

DIRECTIONS
- Mix together the water and sugar in a large sauce pan on medium heat. Allow the mixture to come to a boil. Then lower to low heat, and let the mixture simmer until the sugar dissolve. Allow the mixture to cool completely.

- Mix the lime juice and zest with the cooled mixture.

- Pour the ingredients into the canister, follow the instructions above to set up your ice cream maker, and let it churn for 25-30 minutes.

- Place in an airtight container for up to 2 hours, until desired consistency is reached.

Chunky Cherry Sorbet

This sorbet lets the tart and sweetness of the cherries shine. It goes great with angel food cake.

Prep Time: 2 hours 40 Minutes
Servings: 6

INGREDIENTS
6 cups frozen pitted cherries
1/4 cup sugar
Juice of one lemon

DIRECTIONS
- Puree the sugar and cherries in a food processor or blender until smooth. Put in the lemon juice and pulse a few times to mix the ingredients.

- Pour the ingredients into the canister, follow the instructions above to set up your ice cream maker, and let it churn for 25-30 minutes.

- Place in an airtight container for up to 2 hours, until desired consistency is reached.

Sassy Strawberry Lime Sorbet

This sorbet has a lovely velvety texture. The sweetness of the strawberries is tamed by the citrus flavor of the lime.

Prep Time: 3 hours
Servings: 4

INGREDIENTS
2 cups water
3 pounds chilled strawberries
2 ½ cup sugar
5 chilled limes

DIRECTIONS
- Mix together the water and sugar in a large sauce pan on medium heat. Allow the mixture to come to a boil. Then lower to low heat, and let the mixture simmer until the sugar dissolve. Allow the mixture to cool completely.

- Puree the strawberries in a food processor or blender until smooth. Then add the zest of 3 limes, juice of 5 limes, and the cooled syrup. Blend until all ingredients are mixed.

- Mix the lime juice and zest with the cooled mixture.

- Pour the ingredients into the canister, follow the instructions above to set up your ice cream maker, and let it churn for 25-30 minutes.

- Place in an airtight container for up to 2 hours, until desired consistency is reached.

Samantha Kaine

Something Different

Oh it's different alright! We show you how you can really "Get Jiggy With It!" These amazing delicious flavors will show you how creative you can be with your ice cream desserts. Don't ask questions...just dive in head first! Yumm!

Big Banana Nutella Soft Serve Ice Cream

Nutella is a rich chocolate hazelnut spread that originated in Europe. It pairs well with the sweetness of the bananas.

Prep Time: 35 Minutes
Servings: 6

INGREDIENTS
2 cups heavy cream
1 cup milk
¾ cup sugar
1 Tbs. vanilla extract
1 cup sliced Bananas
6 tbs. Nutella

DIRECTIONS

✦ Place the milk and cream in a bowl, and mix them together until well combined. Use a whisk to mix in the sugar. Continue to whisk for about 4 minutes until the sugar dissolves. Then mix in the vanilla extract.

✦ Place all the ingredients in a food processor or blender, and puree.

✦ Pour the ingredients into the canister, follow the instructions above to set up your ice cream maker, and let it churn for 25 minutes.

✦ Serve immediately.

Chocolate Peanut Butter Soft Serve Ice cream

This ice cream is incredibly rich and creamy. The chocolate adds a lovely richness that combines perfectly with the nutty, creaminess of the peanut butter.

Prep Time: 40 Minutes
Servings: 6

INGREDIENTS
- 2 cups heavy cream
- 1 cup milk
- 3/4 cup sugar
- 1 Tbs. vanilla extract
- 1/2 cup peanut butter slightly melted
- 2 ounces semi-sweet chocolate

DIRECTIONS
- Melt the chocolate in a medium sauce pan on low heat. Allow the chocolate to cool a bit.

- While the chocolate is cooling, place the milk and cream in a bowl, and mix them together until well combined. Use a whisk to mix in the sugar. Continue to whisk for about 4 minutes until the sugar dissolves. Mix in the vanilla extract. Then whisk in the peanut butter, and then the chocolate.

- Pour the ingredients into the canister, follow the instructions above to set up your ice cream maker, and let it churn for 25 minutes.

- Serve immediately.

Basil Soft Serve Ice Cream

This ice cream has an amazing aromatic and fresh flavor. It maintains a sweetness that balances out the aromatic flavor of the basil.

Prep Time: 35 Minutes
Servings: 6

INGREDIENTS
- 2 cups heavy cream
- 1 cup milk
- ¾ cup sugar
- 1 Tbs. vanilla extract
- 1 ½ cups packed basil

DIRECTIONS
- Place the milk and cream in a bowl, and mix them together until well combined. Use a whisk to mix in the sugar. Continue to whisk for about 4 minutes until the sugar dissolves. Mix in the vanilla extract.

- Place all the ingredients in a food processor or blender, and puree.

- Pour the ingredients into the canister, follow the instructions above to set up your ice cream maker, and let it churn for 25 minutes.

- Serve immediately.

"Stuffed" Snickers Soft Serve Ice Cream

You can go buy snickers ice cream bars at a store, but now you can make you own soft serve version. It's nice and creamy with gooey chunks of snickers.

Prep Time: 35 Minutes
Servings: 6

INGREDIENTS
2 cups heavy cream
1 cup milk
¾ cup sugar
1 Tbs. vanilla extract
1 ½ cups chopped mini snickers bars

DIRECTIONS
- Place the milk and cream in a bowl, and mix them together until well combined. Use a whisk to mix in the sugar. Continue to whisk for about 4 minutes until the sugar dissolves. Mix in the vanilla extract.

- Pour all the ingredients into the canister and stir well, follow the instructions above to set up your ice cream maker, and let it churn for 25 minutes.

- Serve immediately.

Matcha Ice Cream

Matcha is a form of ground up green tea. It has a deep, intense tea flavor. Try serving with sweet cookies to if you want to mellow out the flavor.

Prep Time: 2 Hours 50 Minutes
Servings: 6

INGREDIENTS

2 cups heavy cream
1 cup milk
3/4 cup sugar
1 teaspoon vanilla extract
1 tablespoon matcha

DIRECTIONS

✦ Place the milk and cream in a bowl, and mix them together until well combined. Use a whisk to mix in the sugar. Continue to whisk for about 4 minutes until the sugar dissolves. Then mix in the vanilla extract. Finally whisk in the matcha until well mixed.

✦ Pour the ingredients into the canister, follow the instructions above to set up your ice cream maker, and let it churn for 25 minutes.

✦ Put the ice cream in an airtight container and place in the freezer for around 2 hours. Allow the ice cream to thaw for 15 minutes before serving.

Orange Dream Soda Ice Cream

This has all the great taste of your favorite orange soda. It's has a nice creaminess, and is oh so sweet.

Prep Time: 2 Hours 50 Minutes
Servings: 6

INGREDIENTS
2 cups heavy cream
1 cup milk
3/4 cup sugar
1 teaspoon vanilla extract
20 ounces of your favorite orange soda

DIRECTIONS

✦ Place the milk and cream in a bowl, and mix them together until well combined. Use a whisk to mix in the sugar. Continue to whisk for about 4 minutes until the sugar dissolves. Then mix in the vanilla extract and orange soda.

✦ Pour the ingredients into the canister, follow the instructions above to set up your ice cream maker, and let it churn for 25 minutes.

✦ Put the ice cream in an airtight container and place in the freezer for around 2 hours. Allow the ice cream to thaw for 15 minutes before serving.

Aromatic Earl Grey Tea Ice Cream

This ice cream has all the delicious, aromatic flavor of earl grey tea, but with a nice sweetness. Use a high quality tea for this recipe.

Prep Time: 2 Hours 50 Minutes
Servings: 6

INGREDIENTS
   2 cups heavy cream
   1 cup milk
   3/4 cup sugar
   1 teaspoon vanilla extract
   4 tablespoons earl grey tea

DIRECTIONS
- Put the milk in a pan and bring it to a simmer. Add in the tea, take the pot off the heat, and allow to seep for 5 minutes. Discard the tea, and allow milk to cool.

- Place the milk and cream in a bowl, and mix them together until well combined. Use a whisk to mix in the sugar. Continue to whisk for about 4 minutes until the sugar dissolves. Then mix in the vanilla extract.

- Pour the ingredients into the canister, follow the instructions above to set up your ice cream maker, and let it churn for 25 minutes.

- Put the ice cream in an airtight container and place in the freezer for around 2 hours. Allow the ice cream to thaw for 15 minutes before serving.

"Crispy" Kit Kat Ice Cream

This ice cream gets a burst of chocolaty goodness thanks to the Kit Kat. The Kit Kat also gives the ice cream a great crunchy texture.

Prep Time: 2 Hours 50 Minutes
Servings: 6

INGREDIENTS

2 cups heavy cream
1 cup milk
3/4 cup sugar
1 tablespoon vanilla extract
1 ½ cups chopped mini kit kats

DIRECTIONS

- Place the milk and cream in a bowl, and mix them together until well combined. Use a whisk to mix in the sugar. Continue to whisk for about 4 minutes until the sugar dissolves. Then mix in the vanilla extract.

- Pour all the ingredients into the canister and stir well, follow the instructions above to set up your ice cream maker, and let it churn for 25 minutes.

- Put the ice cream in an airtight container and place in the freezer for around 2 hours. Allow the ice cream to thaw for 15 minutes before serving.

Chocolaty Chocolate Pretzel Gelato

The chocolate has a deeply rich base for the gelato. The pretzels give the gelato a lovely saltiness that enhance and balance the chocolate.

Prep Time: 2 Hours 35 Minutes
Servings: 4-6

INGREDIENTS
   1/2 cup heavy cream
   2 cups milk
   3/4 cup sugar
   1 teaspoon vanilla extract
   7 ounces semi-sweet chocolate
   4 ounce pretzels

DIRECTIONS
✦ Melt the chocolate, and allow it to cool a little bit.

✦ Place the milk and cream in a bowl, and mix them together until well combined. Use a whisk to mix in the sugar. Continue to whisk for about 4 minutes until the sugar dissolves. Then mix in the vanilla extract. Finally mix in the chocolate

✦ Place the pretzels in a food processor, and process until the cookies are no bigger than chocolate chips. If you don't have a food processor place the pretzels in a large resealable plastic bag, and seal it shut. Use your hands, a mallet, or a rolling pin to crush the pretzels.

✦ Pour all the ingredients into the canister and stir well, follow the instructions above to set up your ice cream maker, and let it churn for 25 minutes.

✦ Put the gelato in an airtight container and place in the freezer for up to 2 hours, until desired consistency is reached.

Chocolate Matcha Gelato

The matcha has an intense green tea flavor. The chocolate helps to cut through the flavor of the matcha, and adds a deep flavor.

Prep Time: 2 Hours 35 Minutes
Servings: 4-6

INGREDIENTS
1/2 cup heavy cream
2 cups milk
3/4 cup sugar
1 teaspoon vanilla extract

1 tablespoon matcha
2 ounces chopped dark chocolate

DIRECTIONS

- Place the milk and cream in a bowl, and mix them together until well combined. Use a whisk to mix in the sugar. Continue to whisk for about 4 minutes until the sugar dissolves. Then mix in the vanilla extract. Finally whisk in the matcha until well mixed.

- Pour the ingredients into the canister, follow the instructions above to set up your ice cream maker, and let it churn for 25 minutes. About 5 minutes before the ice cream is done churning add the chocolate to your ice cream maker.

- Put the gelato in an airtight container and place in the freezer for up to 2 hours, until desired consistency is reached.

Aromatic Rose Gelato

This gelato has a lovely floral flavor. The rose pairs well with the milk and cream, and creates a delicious gelato.

Prep Time: 2 Hours 35 Minutes
Servings: 4-6

INGREDIENTS
1/2 cup heavy cream
2 cups milk
3/4 cup sugar
1 teaspoon rose extract

DIRECTIONS
- Place the milk and cream in a bowl, and mix them together until well combined. Use a whisk to mix in the sugar. Continue to whisk for about 4 minutes until the sugar dissolves. Then mix in the rose extract.

- Pour the ingredients into the canister, follow the instructions above to set up your ice cream maker, and let it churn for 25 minutes.

- Put the gelato in an airtight container and place in the freezer for up to 2 hours, until desired consistency is reached.

Creamy White Chocolate Rose Frozen Yogurt

This frozen yogurt as a light sweet flavor thanks to the white chocolate. The rose water gives the frozen yogurt a touch of floral flavor.

Prep Time: 2 Hours 35 Minutes
Servings: 1 Quart

INGREDIENTS

1 quart container full-fat plain yogurt
¼ teaspoon salt
1 cup sugar
1 teaspoon vanilla extract
6 ounces chopped white chocolate
½ teaspoon rose water

DIRECTIONS

- Melt the white chocolate and let it cool a bit

- Place the yogurt in a bowl. Use a whisk to mix in the sugar and salt. Continue to whisk for about 4 minutes until the sugar dissolves. Then mix in the vanilla extract, rose water and white chocolate.

- Pour the ingredients into the canister, follow the instructions above to set up your ice cream maker, and let it churn for 25 minutes.

- Put the frozen yogurt in an airtight container and place in the freezer for at least 2 hours, until desired consistency is reached.

Chocolate Olive Oil Frozen Yogurt

You may not think of olive oil as something that goes in dessert, but it adds a nice nutty flavor, and creamy texture. Make sure to use a high quality olive oil.

Prep Time: 2 Hours 35 Minutes
Servings: 1 Quart

INGREDIENTS
   1 quart container full-fat plain yogurt
   ¼ teaspoon salt
   1 cup sugar
   1 teaspoon vanilla extract
   4 ounces chopped dark chocolate
   1/4 cup olive oil

DIRECTIONS
✦ Place the yogurt in a bowl. Use a whisk to mix in the sugar and salt. Continue to whisk for about 4 minutes until the sugar dissolves. Then mix in the vanilla extract, and olive oil.

✦ Pour all the ingredients into the canister and stir well, follow the instructions above to set up your ice cream maker, and let it churn for 25 minutes.

✦ Put the frozen yogurt in an airtight container and place in the freezer for at least 2 hours, until desired consistency is reached.

Sweet Pumpkin Gingerbread Frozen Yogurt

This has all the flavor of wintertime. The ginger and cinnamon give this frozen yogurt a lovely warm flavor.

Prep Time: 2 Hours 35 Minutes
Servings: 1 Quart

INGREDIENTS

1 quart container full-fat plain yogurt
¼ teaspoon salt
1 cup sugar
1 teaspoon vanilla extract
1/2 cup pumpkin
2 tablespoons molasses
1 teaspoon cinnamon
¼ teaspoon ginger

DIRECTIONS

✦ Place all the ingredients in a blender and blend on high until pureed and sugar dissolves.

✦ Pour all the ingredients into the canister and stir well, follow the instructions above to set up your ice cream maker, and let it churn for 25 minutes.

✦ Put the frozen yogurt in an airtight container and place in the freezer for at least 2 hours, until desired consistency is reached.

Finger Lickin' Honey Lavender Milkshake

This milkshake has a delicate flavor that lets the honey take center stage. The lavender gives a subtle floral flower.

Prep Time: 25 Minutes
Servings: 6

INGREDIENTS

2 cups heavy cream
1 cup milk
3/4 cup sugar
1½ teaspoon lavender extract
1/3 cup honey

DIRECTIONS

✦ Place the milk and cream in a bowl, and mix them together until well combined. Use a whisk to mix in the sugar. Continue to whisk for about 4 minutes until the sugar dissolves. Then mix in the lavender extract, and honey.

✦ Pour the ingredients into the canister, follow the instructions above to set up your ice cream maker, and let it churn for 10-15 minutes, until desired consistency is reached.

✦ Serve immediately.

Fun Fig Mint Milkshake

This is a great way to use figs when they're in season. The sweet flavor of the figs is enhanced by the fresh flavor of the mint.

Prep Time: 25 Minutes
Servings: 6

INGREDIENTS
  2 cups heavy cream
  1 cup milk
  3/4 cup sugar
  2 teaspoons vanilla extract
  1/4 cup lemon juice
  2 cups peeled, diced figs
  2 teaspoons chopped fresh mint

DIRECTIONS
- Place the milk and cream in a bowl, and mix them together until well combined. Use a whisk to mix in the sugar. Continue to whisk for about 4 minutes until the sugar dissolves. Then mix in the vanilla extract, lemon juice, and mint.

- Pour all the ingredients into the canister and stir well, follow the instructions above to set up your ice cream maker, and let it churn for 10-15 minutes, until desired consistency is reached.

- Serve immediately.

Mouth Watering Maple Bacon Milkshake

Bacon lovers will go crazy for this shake. The ice cream itself has a lovely maple flavor the goes well with the chunks of bacon.

Prep Time: 25 Minutes
Servings: 6

INGREDIENTS
- 2 cups heavy cream
- 1 cup milk
- 3/4 cup sugar
- 1 teaspoons vanilla extract
- 6 slices finely chopped cooked thick cut bacon
- ½ cup maple syrup

DIRECTIONS
- Place the milk and cream in a bowl, and mix them together until well combined. Use a whisk to mix in the sugar. Continue to whisk for about 4 minutes until the sugar dissolves. Then mix in the vanilla extract, and maple syrup.

- Pour the ingredients into the canister, follow the instructions above to set up your ice cream maker, and let it churn for 10-15 minutes, until desired consistency is reached. About 5 minutes before the ice cream is done churning add the bacon to your ice cream maker.

- Serve immediately.

Plum Sorbet

The plums give this sorbet an interesting sweet yet tart flavor. Try combining different types of plums to make a more complex flavor.

Prep Time: 4 hours 35 Minutes
Servings: Makes 1 Quart

INGREDIENTS
2 pounds pitted, quartered plums
1 tablespoon light corn syrup
1 cup sugar
¼ teaspoon salt

DIRECTIONS
- Use a food processor or blender to puree the plums. Put in the sugar and corn syrup, and process for about another 30 seconds. Then blend in the salt. Strain the mixture into a bowl, and refrigerate covered for 2-3 hours.

- Pour the ingredients into the canister, follow the instructions above to set up your ice cream maker, and let it churn for 25-30 minutes.

- Place in an airtight container for up to 2 hours, until desired consistency is reached.

Clementine Sorbet

This sorbet has a beautiful orange color. The sweet taste of the clementine sorbet taste best the day it's made.

Prep Time: 4 hours 35 Minutes
Servings: Makes 1 Quart

INGREDIENTS
20 chilled, peeled, and segmented clementines

1 cup sugar
¼ teaspoon salt

DIRECTIONS
- Use a food processor or blender to puree the clementines. Strain the puree until you have 4 ½ cups of juice. Place the juice and sugar back in the blender or food processor. Process until sugar dissolves. Then pulse in the salt until combined.

- Pour the ingredients into the canister, follow the instructions above to set up your ice cream maker, and let it churn for 25-30 minutes.

- Place in an airtight container for up to 2 hours, until desired consistency is reached.

Luscious Lavender Sour Cherry Sorbet

This sorbet has a lovely sour flavor with a hint of floral flavor from the lavender. If the base seems a little too sour know that it will mellow out a bit when it's frozen.

Prep Time: 5 hours 35 Minutes
Servings: 6

INGREDIENTS
3 cups pitted, sliced sour cherries
½ teaspoon lavender
3/4 cup sugar
1/2 teaspoon salt
2 tablespoons vanilla extract
2 ½ teaspoons lime juice

DIRECTIONS

✦ Use a food processor or blender to puree the lavender, sugar, cherries, and vanilla extract. Then blend in the salt and lime juice. Strain the mixture into a bowl, and refrigerate covered for 2-3 hours.

✦ Pour the ingredients into the canister, follow the instructions above to set up your ice cream maker, and let it churn for 25-30 minutes.

✦ Place in an airtight container for up to 2 hours, until desired consistency is reached.

Mango Madness Chili Lime Sorbet

This sorbet combines three different flavors that go so well together. The mango gives it a sweet creamy flavor, the lime adds some tartness, and the chili powder adds just a little heat.

Prep Time: 2 hours 40 Minutes
Servings: 6-8

INGREDIENTS
3 peeled, pitted, and diced large mangos
1 tablespoon chili powder
2 cups simple syrup
1/4 cup fresh lime juice
Pinch of salt

DIRECTIONS
✦ Puree the mangos in a food processor or blender. Then add in the remaining ingredients and blend on low until combined.

✦ Pour the ingredients into the canister, follow the instructions above to set up your ice cream maker, and let it churn for 25-30 minutes.

✦ Place in an airtight container for up to 2 hours, until desired consistency is reached.

Lingering Lemon Mint Sorbet

This sorbet combines three different flavors that go so well together. The mango gives it a sweet creamy flavor, the lime adds some tartness, and the chili powder adds just a little heat.

Prep Time: 3 hours 10 Minutes
Servings: 4

INGREDIENTS
½ cup lemon juice
1 cup boiling water
1 cup chopped mint
Zest of 1 lemon
1 cup sugar

DIRECTIONS
- Mix together the sugar, lemon zest, and mint in a heat safe bowl. Then pour in the water, and stir frequently until sugar dissolves. Let the mixture sit for 20 minutes. Then strain it into another bowl. Mix in the lemon juice and let the mixture cool totally.

- Pour the ingredients into the canister, follow the instructions above to set up your ice cream maker, and let it churn for 25-30 minutes.

- Place in an airtight container for up to 2 hours, until desired consistency is reached.

Our Complete Hamilton Beach® Ice Cream Recipe Book

On The Healthy Side

Like we said...You don't have to feel soo darn guilty! This section will bring you back to the dessert world! "Without all of the guilt" and still Mmmmmm sooo gooooood! Enjoy!

Vegan Chocolate Soft Serve Ice cream

This ice cream gets its creaminess from the coconut milk or cream. It has a deep rich chocolate flavor that rivals any traditional ice cream.

Prep Time: 50 Minutes
Cook Time: 10 Minutes
Servings: 9

INGREDIENTS
3/4 cup water
1 1/4 cups full fat coconut milk or coconut cream (thick as possible)
2/3 cup organic cane sugar
2/3 cup unsweetened cocoa powder
1/4 tsp sea salt
6 ounces vegan dark chocolate, finely chopped
1/2 tsp pure vanilla extract

DIRECTIONS

✦ Put the first 5 ingredients in a large saucepan, and heat it on medium-high heat. Mix the ingredients together using a whisk. Allow the mixture to come to a low boil. Continue to whisk often, and remain cooking on a low boil for 1 minute.

✦ Take the pan off the heat, and mix in the chocolate and vanilla extract using the whisk. Continue to mix until the chocolate is melted.

✦ Place the mixture in a blender, and blend on high speed for about 30 seconds.

✦ Allow the mixture to cool

✦ Pour the ingredients into the canister, follow the instructions above to set up your ice cream maker, and let it churn for 25 minutes.

✦ Serve immediately.

Vegan Radical Raspberry Chocolate Soft Serve Ice Cream

This ice cream has a deeply rich chocolate flavor. The raspberry gives this ice cream a lovely sweetness that balances out the rich flavor of the chocolate.

Prep Time: 50 Minutes
Cook Time: 10 Minutes
Servings: 9

INGREDIENTS
- 3/4 cup water
- 1 1/4 cups full fat coconut milk or coconut cream (as thick as possible)
- 2/3 cup organic cane sugar
- 2/3 cup unsweetened cocoa powder
- 1/4 tsp sea salt
- 6 ounces vegan dark chocolate, finely chopped
- 1/2 tsp pure vanilla extract
- 1/2 cup raspberries

DIRECTIONS
- Put the first 5 ingredients in a large saucepan, and heat it on medium-high heat. Mix the ingredients together using a whisk. Allow the mixture to come to a low boil. Continue to whisk often, and remain cooking on a low boil for 1 minute.
- Take the pan off the heat, and mix in the chocolate and vanilla extract using the whisk. Continue to mix until the chocolate is melted.
- Place the mixture in a blender with the raspberries, and blend on high speed for about 30 seconds or until the raspberries are pureed.
- Allow the mixture to cool
- Pour the ingredients into the canister, follow the instructions above to set up your ice cream maker, and let it churn for 25 minutes.
- Serve immediately.

Vegan "Oh So" Soy Vanilla Soft Serve Ice Cream

The tofu, and coconut milk give this ice cream a rich texture. Although it's vegan, this ice cream still has all the great taste of traditional ice cream.

Prep Time: 35 Minutes
Servings: Makes 1 Quart

INGREDIENTS
- 1 pound silken tofu
- ½ cup plus 2 tablespoons organic or granulated sugar
- ½ teaspoon kosher salt
- 1 vanilla bean, split lengthwise
- ¾ cup refined coconut oil, melted, cooled slightly

DIRECTIONS
- Put the first 3 ingredients in a blender. Then add in the vanilla bean seeds. Puree the mixture until its smooth, around 15 seconds. Turn the blender to medium speed, and slowly drizzle in the coconut oil. Blend the mixture until its thick, but don't over blend it.

- Pour the ingredients into the canister, follow the instructions above to set up your ice cream maker, and let it churn for 25 minutes.

- Serve immediately.

Vegan Chunky Chocolate Almond Ice cream

This Ice cream has a deep, rich chocolate flavor that matches any traditional ice cream. The almonds give a nice crunch, and a nutty flavor that enhances the chocolate.

Prep Time: 3 Hours 15 Minutes
Cook Time: 10 Minutes
Servings: 9

INGREDIENTS
>3/4 cup water
>1 1/4 cups full fat coconut milk or coconut cream (as thick as possible)
>2/3 cup organic cane sugar
>2/3 cup unsweetened cocoa powder
>1/4 tsp sea salt
>6 ounces vegan dark chocolate, finely chopped
>1/2 tsp pure vanilla extract
>½ cup chopped almonds

DIRECTIONS
- Put the first 5 ingredients in a large saucepan, and heat it on medium-high heat. Mix the ingredients together using a whisk. Allow the mixture to come to a low boil. Continue to whisk often, and remain cooking on a low boil for 1 minute.

- Take the pan off the heat, and mix in the chocolate and vanilla extract using the whisk. Continue to mix until the chocolate is melted.

- Place the mixture in a blender, and blend on high speed for about 30 seconds.

- Allow the mixture to cool

- Pour all the ingredients into the canister and stir well, follow the instructions above to set up your ice cream maker, and let it churn for 25 minutes.

- Put the ice cream in an airtight container and place in the freezer for around 2 hours. Allow the ice cream to thaw for 15 min.

Vegan Sensuous Strawberries N Cream Ice Cream

The tofu, and coconut milk give this ice cream a rich texture. Although it's vegan, this ice cream still has all the great taste of traditional ice cream.

Prep Time: 35 Minutes
Servings: Makes 1 Quart

INGREDIENTS
1 pound silken tofu
½ cup plus 2 tablespoons organic or granulated sugar
½ teaspoon kosher salt
1 vanilla bean, split lengthwise
¾ cup refined coconut oil, melted, cooled slightly
1 cup sliced strawberries

DIRECTIONS
✦ Put the first 3 ingredients in a blender. Then add in the vanilla bean seeds and strawberries. Puree the mixture until its smooth, around 15 seconds. Turn the blender to medium speed, and slowly drizzle in the coconut oil. Blend the mixture until its thick, but don't over blend it.

✦ Pour all the ingredients into the canister and stir well, follow the instructions above to set up your ice cream maker, and let it churn for 25 minutes.

✦ Put the ice cream in an airtight container and place in the freezer for around 2 hours. Allow the ice cream to thaw for 15 minutes before serving.

Vegan Soy Vanilla And Carob Chip Ice Cream

The tofu, and coconut milk give this ice cream a rich texture. Although it's vegan, this ice cream still has all the great taste of traditional ice cream.

Prep Time: 35 Minutes
Servings: Makes 1 Quart

INGREDIENTS
- 1 pound silken tofu
- ½ cup plus 2 tablespoons organic or granulated sugar
- ½ teaspoon kosher salt
- 1 vanilla bean, split lengthwise
- ¾ cup refined coconut oil, melted, cooled slightly
- 1 cup vegan carob chips

DIRECTIONS
- Put the first 3 ingredients in a blender. Then add in the vanilla bean seeds. Puree the mixture until its smooth, around 15 seconds. Turn the blender to medium speed, and slowly drizzle in the coconut oil. Blend the mixture until its thick, but don't over blend it.

- Pour all the ingredients into the canister and stir well, follow the instructions above to set up your ice cream maker, and let it churn for 25 minutes.

- Put the ice cream in an airtight container and place in the freezer for around 2 hours. Allow the ice cream to thaw for 15 minutes before serving.

Vegan Pistachio "Punch" Chocolate Chunk Gelato

This gelato is packed with nutty pistachio taste. The chocolate adds depth of flavor and a crunchy texture.

Prep Time: 2 Hours 35 Minutes
Servings: 4

INGREDIENTS
2 cups shelled, roasted, salted pistachios
1 can coconut milk
1/2 cup arrowroot
¾ cup sugar
1 teaspoon lime juice
4 ounces chopped vegan chocolate

DIRECTIONS
- Pulse the pistachios in a food processor for about 3 minutes
- Place all ingredients EXCEPT the chocolate in a blender. Blend on high speed until smooth.
- Pour all the ingredients into the canister and stir well, follow the instructions above to set up your ice cream maker, and let it churn for 25 minutes.
- Put the gelato in an airtight container and place in the freezer for up to 2 hours, until desired consistency is reached.

Vegan Sweet Chocolate Strawberry Chunk Gelato

This gelato has a rich chocolaty taste that gets its great texture from the coconut cream, and frozen bananas. The strawberries give a sweet burst in the middle of the deep chocolate gelato.

Prep Time: 2 Hours 35 Minutes
Servings: Makes 2 ½ cups

INGREDIENTS

1 cup refrigerated coconut cream
1 cup pitted dates
1 cup frozen banana pieces

3 tablespoons cocoa powder
1/2 teaspoon salt
½ cup strawberry cut into chunk

DIRECTIONS

✦ Place all ingredients EXCEPT the strawberries in a blender. Blend on high speed until smooth.

✦ Pour all the ingredients into the canister and stir well, follow the instructions above to set up your ice cream maker, and let it churn for 25 minutes.

✦ Put the gelato in an airtight container and place in the freezer for up to 2 hours, until desired consistency is reached.

Samantha Kaine

Vegan Big Blackberry Soy Frozen Yogurt

This easy to make frozen yogurt starts with a soy yogurt, and adds blackberry jam for flavor. Make sure to use a high quality jam.

Prep Time: 2 Hours 30 Minutes
Servings: 1 Quart

INGREDIENTS
2 ¾ cups unsweetened plain soy yogurt
1¼ blackberry jam

DIRECTIONS
- Place the yogurt in a bowl and mix in the jam. Use a hand mixer to beat the mixture for 5 minutes.

- Pour the ingredients into the canister, follow the instructions above to set up your ice cream maker, and let it churn for 25 minutes.

- Put the frozen yogurt in an airtight container and place in the freezer for at least 2 hours, until desired consistency is reached.

Vegan Ridiculous Raspberry Coconut Frozen Yogurt

This frozen yogurt combines the sweet flavor of raspberry with the tropical rich flavor of coconut. Try covering it with vegan chocolate sauce for even more flavor.

Prep Time: 2 Hours 35 Minutes
Servings: 1 Quart

INGREDIENTS
2 cups coconut yogurt
1/4 cup sugar or maple syrup
1/2 teaspoon vanilla extract
1/4 cup shredded coconut
½ cup raspberries

DIRECTIONS

- Puree the raspberries in a food processor or blender.

- Place the yogurt in a bowl. Use a whisk to mix in the sugar. Continue to whisk for about 4 minutes until the sugar dissolves. Then mix in the vanilla extract, and raspberry puree.

- Pour all the ingredients into the canister and stir well, follow the instructions above to set up your ice cream maker, and let it churn for 25 minutes.

- Put the frozen yogurt in an airtight container and place in the freezer for at least 2 hours, until desired consistency is reached.

Vegan Chunky Chocolate Banana Milkshake

This taste like a creamy version of a chocolate covered banana. It's got a good balance of chocolate and banana flavor.

Prep Time: 40 Minutes
Cook Time: 10 Minutes
Servings: 9

INGREDIENTS

3/4 cup water
1 1/4 cups full fat coconut milk or coconut cream (as thick as possible)
2/3 cup organic cane sugar
2/3 cup unsweetened cocoa powder
1/4 tsp sea salt
6 ounces vegan dark chocolate, finely chopped
1/2 tsp pure vanilla extract
½ cup sliced frozen bananas

DIRECTIONS

- Put the first 5 ingredients in a large saucepan, and heat it on medium-high heat. Mix the ingredients together using a whisk. Allow the mixture to come to a low boil. Continue to whisk often, and remain cooking on a low boil for 1 minute.

- Take the pan off the heat, and mix in the chocolate and vanilla extract using the whisk. Continue to mix until the chocolate is melted.

- Place the mixture in a blender with the bananas, and blend on high speed for about 30 seconds.

- Allow the mixture to cool

- Pour the ingredients into the canister, follow the instructions above to set up your ice cream maker, and let it churn for 10-15 minutes, until desired consistency is reached.

- Serve immediately.

Vegan Chocolate Made Mint Milkshake

Mint and chocolate go so well together in any form. The freshness of the mint compliments the rich complex flavor of the chocolate

Prep Time: 40 Minutes
Cook Time: 10 Minutes
Servings: 9

INGREDIENTS
3/4 cup water
1 1/4 cups full fat coconut milk or coconut cream (as thick as possible)
2/3 cup organic cane sugar
2/3 cup unsweetened cocoa powder
1/4 tsp sea salt
6 ounces vegan dark chocolate, finely chopped
1 1/2 tsp mint extract
½ cup sliced frozen bananas

DIRECTIONS
✦ Put the first 5 ingredients in a large saucepan, and heat it on medium-high heat. Mix the ingredients together using a whisk. Allow the mixture to come to a low boil. Continue to whisk often, and remain cooking on a low boil for 1 minute.

✦ Take the pan off the heat, and mix in the chocolate and mint extract using the whisk. Continue to mix until the chocolate is melted.

✦ Place the mixture in a blender with the bananas, and blend on high speed for about 30 seconds.

✦ Allow the mixture to cool

✦ Pour the ingredients into the canister, follow the instructions above to set up your ice cream maker, and let it churn for 10-15 minutes, until desired consistency is reached.

✦ Serve immediately.

Wonderful Watermelon Sorbet

This is a great dessert after a heavy meal. It's light, refreshing, and a great pallet cleanser.

Prep Time: 2 hours 40 Minutes
Servings: Makes 1 Quart

INGREDIENTS
3 1/2 cups sliced seedless watermelon
6 ounce chilled pineapple juice
3/4 cup chilled ginger ale
½ cup fresh lime juice
1/3 cup grenadine

DIRECTIONS
- Puree all ingredients in a food processor or blender.

- Pour the ingredients into the canister, follow the instructions above to set up your ice cream maker, and let it churn for 25-30 minutes.

- Place in an airtight container for up to 2 hours, until desired consistency is reached.

Deep Dark Chocolate Sorbet

This has a great chocolate taste, that's also healthy. Cocoa powder is packed with antioxidants and ¾ cup of sweetener keeps the calories down.

Prep Time: 5 hours
Servings: 3

INGREDIENTS
- 2 cups water
- 1 cup unsweetened cocoa powder
- 3/4 cup agave
- 1 tablespoon lime zest

DIRECTIONS
- Mix together the water and agave in a medium saucepan on medium heat. Stir frequently until the agave dissolve. Mix in the cocoa powder and let the mixture come to a simmer. Let the mixture cook for 3 minutes. Allow the mixture to cool completely. Then refrigerate covered for 2 hours.

- Pour the ingredients into the canister, follow the instructions above to set up your ice cream maker, and let it churn for 25-30 minutes.

- Place in an airtight container for up to 2 hours, until desired consistency is reached.

Samantha Kaine

Child's Play

✦ Who said you have to grow up so fast? Awesome section for the kiddos and great for those times when the young'ins need a nice treat

Kiddo's Coca Cola Soft Serve Ice Cream

This ice cream has all the delicious flavor coca cola, but with the creaminess of ice cream. Imagine having your coke float in an ice cream form, and this is what you get.

Prep Time: 55 Minutes
Servings: 6

INGREDIENTS
- 2 cups heavy cream
- 1 cup milk
- ¾ cup sugar
- 1 Tbs. vanilla extract
- 3 cups coca cola (2, 12 ounce cans)

DIRECTIONS

- Pour the coke into a large skillet, and heat it on high heat until it comes to a boil. Allow the coke to cook for about another 15 or 20 minutes, until the coke reduces down to 1 cup of liquid. Let the liquid cool.

- Place the milk and cream in a bowl, and mix them together until well combined. Use a whisk to mix in the sugar. Continue to whisk for about 4 minutes until the sugar dissolves. Mix in the vanilla extract, and then the reduced coca cola.

- Pour the ingredients into the canister, follow the instructions above to set up your ice cream maker, and let it churn for 25 minutes.

- Serve immediately.

Double Bubble Gum Soft Serve Ice Cream

Kids will love everything about this ice cream. Not only does the ice cream taste like bubble gum, it has actual gum balls in it.

Prep Time: 35 Minutes
Servings: 6

INGREDIENTS
- 2 cups heavy cream
- 1 cup milk
- ¾ cup sugar
- 1 Tbs. vanilla extract
- 1 dram bubble gum flavoring
- ½ cup mini gum balls

DIRECTIONS

✦ Place the milk and cream in a bowl, and mix them together until well combined. Use a whisk to mix in the sugar. Continue to whisk for about 4 minutes until the sugar dissolves. Mix in the vanilla extract, and then the bubble gum flavoring.

✦ Pour all the ingredients into the canister and stir well, follow the instructions above to set up your ice cream maker, and let it churn for 25 minutes.

✦ Serve immediately.

"Cool" Cake Batter Soft Serve Ice Cream

Now your kids can have cake and ice cream in one delicious dessert. Using cake batter in the ice cream process makes this ice cream taste just like cake.

Prep Time: 35 Minutes
Servings: 6

INGREDIENTS
   2 cups heavy cream
   1 cup milk
   ¾ cup sugar
   1 Tbs. vanilla extract
   2/3 cup cake mix

DIRECTIONS
+ Place the milk and cream in a bowl, and mix them together until well combined. Use a whisk to mix in the sugar. Continue to whisk for about 4 minutes until the sugar dissolves. Mix in the vanilla extract, and then the 2/3 cup cake mix.

+ Pour the ingredients into the canister, follow the instructions above to set up your ice cream maker, and let it churn for 25 minutes.

+ Serve immediately.

Caramel Corn Soft Serve Ice Cream

Kids will love having two of their favorite sweets combined together. Adding the caramel corn in two different places gives the ice cream texture, and so much caramel corn flavor.

Prep Time: 35 Minutes
Servings: 6

INGREDIENTS
2 cups heavy cream
1 cup milk
¾ cup sugar
1 Tbs. vanilla extract
2 cup caramel corn

DIRECTIONS
✦ Place the milk and cream in a bowl, and mix them together until well combined. Use a whisk to mix in the sugar. Continue to whisk for about 4 minutes until the sugar dissolves. Mix in the vanilla extract. Place the mixture in a blender or food processor with 1 cup of the caramel corn, and puree.

✦ Put the remaining caramel corn in a resealable plastic bag, and seal it. Crush the caramel corn using your hands, or a mallet.

✦ Pour all the ingredients into the canister and stir well, follow the instructions above to set up your ice cream maker, and let it churn for 25 minutes.

✦ Serve immediately.

My Delicious M&M Ice Cream

This ice cream is super colorful thanks to the M&M's. It has a great balance of crunchy chocolate, and vanilla flavor that kids will love.

Prep Time: 2 Hours 50 Minutes
Servings: 6

INGREDIENTS
2 cups heavy cream
1 cup milk
3/4 cup sugar
1 tablespoon vanilla extract
1 ½ cups M&Ms candy

DIRECTIONS

- Place the milk and cream in a bowl, and mix them together until well combined. Use a whisk to mix in the sugar. Continue to whisk for about 4 minutes until the sugar dissolves. Then mix in the vanilla extract.

- Pour all the ingredients into the canister and stir well, follow the instructions above to set up your ice cream maker, and let it churn for 25 minutes.

- Put the ice cream in an airtight container and place in the freezer for around 2 hours. Allow the ice cream to thaw for 15 minutes before serving.

Screamin' Sour Patch Kids Ice Cream

This ice cream is sweet and sour all at once. It has a sweet vanilla base that is contrasted with the delicious sour flavor of the sour patch kids.

Prep Time: 2 Hours 50 Minutes
Servings: 6

INGREDIENTS
2 cups heavy cream
1 cup milk
3/4 cup sugar
1 tablespoon vanilla extract
1 cups chopped sour patch kids

DIRECTIONS
- Place the milk and cream in a bowl, and mix them together until well combined. Use a whisk to mix in the sugar. Continue to whisk for about 4 minutes until the sugar dissolves. Then mix in the vanilla extract.

- Pour all the ingredients into the canister and stir well, follow the instructions above to set up your ice cream maker, and let it churn for 25 minutes.

- Put the ice cream in an airtight container and place in the freezer for around 2 hours. Allow the ice cream to thaw for 15 minutes before serving.

Dr. Pepper Ice Cream

This has all of the delicious flavor of Dr. Pepper in a delicious creamy form. Try making a Sunday with it instead of using vanilla ice cream.

Prep Time: 2 Hours 50 Minutes
Servings: 6

INGREDIENTS
2 cups heavy cream
1 cup milk
3/4 cup sugar
1 tablespoon vanilla extract
3 cups (2, 12 ounce cans) dr. pepper

DIRECTIONS
- Pour the dr. pepper into a large skillet, and heat it on high heat until it comes to a boil. Allow the coke to cook for about another 15 or 20 minutes, until the root beer reduces down to 1 cup of liquid. Let the liquid cool.

- Place the milk and cream in a bowl, and mix them together until well combined. Use a whisk to mix in the sugar. Continue to whisk for about 4 minutes until the sugar dissolves. Then mix in the vanilla extract and dr. pepper reduction.

- Pour the ingredients into the canister, follow the instructions above to set up your ice cream maker, and let it churn for 25 minutes.

- Put the ice cream in an airtight container and place in the freezer for around 2 hours. Allow the ice cream to thaw for 15 minutes before serving.

Samantha Kaine

Radical Root Beer Gelato

This has all the delicious flavor of root beer, but it's oh so creamy. Try making a root beer float with it for double the root beer flavor.

Prep Time: 2 Hours 50 Minutes
Servings: 4-6

INGREDIENTS
1/2 cup heavy cream
2 cups milk
3/4 cup sugar
1 teaspoon vanilla extract
3 cups (2, 12 ounce cans) root beer

DIRECTIONS
- Pour the root beer into a large skillet, and heat it on high heat until it comes to a boil. Allow the coke to cook for about another 15 or 20 minutes, until the root beer reduces down to 1 cup of liquid. Let the liquid cool.

- Place the milk and cream in a bowl, and mix them together until well combined. Use a whisk to mix in the sugar. Continue to whisk for about 4 minutes until the sugar dissolves. Then mix in the vanilla extract and root beer reduction.

- Pour the ingredients into the canister, follow the instructions above to set up your ice cream maker, and let it churn for 25 minutes.

- Put the gelato in an airtight container and place in the freezer for up to 2 hours, until desired consistency is reached.

Three Musketeer Gelato

The vanilla base lets the three musketeers shine. You get tons of creamy, chocolatey flavor in every bite.

Prep Time: 2 Hours 35 Minutes
Servings: 4-6

INGREDIENTS
1/2 cup heavy cream
2 cups milk
3/4 cup sugar
1 tablespoon vanilla extract
1 ½ cups chopped mini three musketeers bars

DIRECTIONS
- Place the milk and cream in a bowl, and mix them together until well combined. Use a whisk to mix in the sugar. Continue to whisk for about 4 minutes until the sugar dissolves. Then mix in the vanilla extract.

- Pour all the ingredients into the canister and stir well, follow the instructions above to set up your ice cream maker, and let it churn for 25 minutes.

- Put the gelato in an airtight container and place in the freezer for up to 2 hours, until desired consistency is reached.

Crunchy Cinnamon Butterfinger Gelato

The vanilla base lets the cinnamon and butterfinger shine through. The cinnamon adds depth of flavor to the butterfinger.

Prep Time: 2 Hours 35 Minutes
Servings: 4-6

INGREDIENTS

1/2 cup heavy cream
2 cups milk
3/4 cup sugar
1 teaspoon vanilla extract
1 ½ cups chopped mini butterfinger bars
2 teaspoons ground cinnamon

DIRECTIONS

✦ Place the milk and cream in a bowl, and mix them together until well combined. Use a whisk to mix in the sugar. Continue to whisk for about 4 minutes until the sugar dissolves. Then mix in the vanilla extract and cinnamon.

✦ Pour all the ingredients into the canister and stir well, follow the instructions above to set up your ice cream maker, and let it churn for 25 minutes.

✦ Put the gelato in an airtight container and place in the freezer for up to 2 hours, until desired consistency is reached.

"Give Me More" S'mores Frozen Yogurt

This has all the flavor of the fireside favorite. If you want a more authentic flavor lightly toast the marshmallows before using.

Prep Time: 2 Hours 35 Minutes
Servings: 1 Quart

INGREDIENTS
- 1 quart container full-fat plain yogurt
- ¼ teaspoon salt
- 1 cup sugar
- 1 teaspoon vanilla extract
- 3 large graham crackers
- 4 ounces chopped semi-sweet chocolate
- ½ cup mini marshmallows

DIRECTIONS
- Place the yogurt in a bowl. Use a whisk to mix in the sugar and salt. Continue to whisk for about 4 minutes until the sugar dissolves. Then mix in the vanilla extract.

- Place the graham crackers in a food processor, and process until the crackers are no bigger than chocolate chips. If you don't have a food processor place the crackers in a large resealable plastic bag, and seal it shut. Use your hands, a mallet, or a rolling pin to crush the cookies.

- Pour all the ingredients into the canister and stir well, follow the instructions above to set up your ice cream maker, and let it churn for 25 minutes.

- Put the frozen yogurt in an airtight container and place in the freezer for at least 2 hours, until desired consistency is reached.

Chilled Cherry Soda Frozen Yogurt

Enjoy all the sweet flavor of cherry soda in this soft and creamy form. Kids will love the red color of this frozen yogurt too!

Prep Time: 2 Hours 50 Minutes
Servings: 1 Quart

INGREDIENTS
  1 quart container full-fat plain yogurt
  ¼ teaspoon salt
  1 cup sugar
  1 teaspoon vanilla extract
  3 cups (2, 12 ounce cans) cherry soda

DIRECTIONS
- Pour the cherry soda into a large skillet, and heat it on high heat until it comes to a boil. Allow the coke to cook for about another 15 or 20 minutes, until the root beer reduces down to 1 cup of liquid. Let the liquid cool.

- Place the yogurt in a bowl. Use a whisk to mix in the sugar and salt. Continue to whisk for about 4 minutes until the sugar dissolves. Then mix in the vanilla extract, and reduced cherry soda.

- Pour the ingredients into the canister, follow the instructions above to set up your ice cream maker, and let it churn for 25 minutes.

- Put the frozen yogurt in an airtight container and place in the freezer for at least 2 hours, until desired consistency is reached.

Cookies 'N Cream Rice Crispy Treat Frozen Yogurt

Kids will go crazy for two delicious treats in one. Not only are they getting cookies 'n cream frozen yogurt, they get the sweet gooey taste of rice crispy treats too.

Prep Time: 2 Hours 35 Minutes
Servings: 1 Quart

INGREDIENTS

1 quart container full-fat plain yogurt
¼ teaspoon salt
1 cup sugar
1 teaspoon vanilla extract
10 chocolate sandwich cookies
1/2 cup rice crispy treats

DIRECTIONS

✦ Place the yogurt in a bowl. Use a whisk to mix in the sugar and salt. Continue to whisk for about 4 minutes until the sugar dissolves. Then mix in the vanilla extract.

✦ Place the sandwich cookies in a food processor, and process until the cookies are no bigger than chocolate chips. If you don't have a food processor place the cookies in a large resealable plastic bag, and seal it shut. Use your hands, a mallet, or a rolling pin to crush the cookies.

✦ Pour all the ingredients into the canister and stir well, follow the instructions above to set up your ice cream maker, and let it churn for 25 minutes.

✦ Put the frozen yogurt in an airtight container and place in the freezer for at least 2 hours, until desired consistency is reached.

Red Velvet Milkshake

This has all the flavor of red velvet cake, but it's so creamy and delicious. Try it with a slice of red velvet cake for a double dose of red velvet.

Prep Time: 25 Minutes
Servings: 6

INGREDIENTS
- 2 cups heavy cream
- 1 cup milk
- 3/4 cup sugar
- 1 teaspoons vanilla extract
- 1 8 ounce package cream cheese, softened
- 1 tablespoon cocoa powder
- 1 tablespoon plus 1 teaspoon red food coloring

DIRECTIONS

✦ Place the milk and cream in a bowl, and mix them together until well combined. Use a whisk to mix in the sugar. Continue to whisk for about 4 minutes until the sugar dissolves. Put all the ingredients in a blender and pulse for around 30 seconds until well mixed.

✦ Pour the ingredients into the canister, follow the instructions above to set up your ice cream maker, and let it churn for 10-15 minutes, until desired consistency is reached.

✦ Serve immediately.

Peanut Butter Cup Milkshake

The vanilla flavor of the ice cream allows the peanut butter cup to shine. Each bite is packed with chocolate peanut butter goodness.

Prep Time: 25 Minutes
Servings: 6

INGREDIENTS
- 2 cups heavy cream
- 1 cup milk
- 3/4 cup sugar
- 1 tablespoon vanilla extract
- 1 1/2 cups chopped mini peanut butter cups
- ½ cup maple syrup

DIRECTIONS
- Place the milk and cream in a bowl, and mix them together until well combined. Use a whisk to mix in the sugar. Continue to whisk for about 4 minutes until the sugar dissolves. Then mix in the vanilla extract.

- Pour all the ingredients into the canister and stir well, follow the instructions above to set up your ice cream maker, and let it churn for 10-15 minutes, until desired consistency is reached.

- Serve immediately.

Crazy Cotton Candy Milkshake

The vanilla flavor of the ice cream allows the peanut butter cup to shine. Each bite is packed with chocolate peanut butter goodness.

Prep Time: 25 Minutes
Servings: 6

INGREDIENTS
2 cups heavy cream
1 cup milk
3/4 cup sugar
1 teaspoon vanilla extract
1/2 cup cotton candy syrup
1 tablespoon plus 1 teaspoon pink or blue food coloring

DIRECTIONS
- Place the milk and cream in a bowl, and mix them together until well combined. Use a whisk to mix in the sugar. Continue to whisk for about 4 minutes until the sugar dissolves. Then mix in the vanilla extract, syrup, and food coloring.

- Pour the ingredients into the canister, follow the instructions above to set up your ice cream maker, and let it churn for 10-15 minutes, until desired consistency is reached.

- Serve immediately.

Island Coconut Banana Sorbet

This sorbet has a lovely tropical flavor. The mellow flavor the banana melds perfectly with creaminess of the coconut.

Prep Time: 2 hours 40 Minutes
Servings: 4-8

INGREDIENTS
3 peeled, mashed bananas
2-4 tablespoons honey to taste
1 1/2 cups light coconut milk
1 teaspoon vanilla extract

DIRECTIONS
✦ Puree all ingredients in a food processor or blender. Taste, and add more honey if desired.

✦ Pour the ingredients into the canister, follow the instructions above to set up your ice cream maker, and let it churn for 25-30 minutes.

✦ Place in an airtight container for up to 2 hours, until desired consistency is reached.

Samantha Kaine

Grown Ups Only!

All I have to say is...Grown Ups can play to! ;) Indulge yourself in these amazingly flavored spiked desserts that will leave you speechless! Great for any occasion...just use your imagination and run with it!

Double Gin And Tonic Soft Serve Ice Cream

Now your kids can have cake and ice cream in one delicious dessert. Using cake batter in the ice cream process makes this ice cream taste just like cake.

Prep Time: 35 Minutes
Servings: 6

INGREDIENTS
2 cups heavy cream
1 cup milk
¾ cup sugar
1 Tbs. vanilla extract
4 tablespoons gin
125 ML tonic water

DIRECTIONS

✦ Place the milk and cream in a bowl, and mix them together until well combined. Use a whisk to mix in the sugar. Continue to whisk for about 4 minutes until the sugar dissolves. Mix in the vanilla extract. Then whisk in the gin and tonic

✦ Pour the ingredients into the canister, follow the instructions above to set up your ice cream maker, and let it churn for 25 minutes.

✦ Serve immediately.

Margarita Madness Soft Serve Ice Cream

This ice cream lets you enjoy all the delicious flavor of a margarita in frozen, creamy form. Try serving is in a salt rimmed dish for the full margarita effect.

Prep Time: 35 Minutes
Servings: 6

INGREDIENTS
2 cups heavy cream
1 cup milk
3/4 cup sugar
1 Tbs. vanilla extract
3 tablespoons tequila
1/2 cup lime juice
2 tablespoons orange liqueur

DIRECTIONS

✦ Place the milk and cream in a bowl, and mix them together until well combined. Use a whisk to mix in the sugar. Continue to whisk for about 4 minutes until the sugar dissolves. Mix in the vanilla extract. Finally whisk in the lime juice, tequila, and liqueur.

✦ Pour the ingredients into the canister, follow the instructions above to set up your ice cream maker, and let it churn for 25 minutes.

✦ Serve immediately.

Vanilla Screwdriver Soft Serve Ice Cream

This has all the sweetness of a screwdriver with the right amount of kick. It's perfect for a party on a hot summer day.

Prep Time: 35 Minutes
Servings: 6

INGREDIENTS
2 cups heavy cream
1 cup milk
¾ cup sugar
1 Tbs. vanilla extract
½ cup orange juice
3 tablespoons vodka

DIRECTIONS

✦ Place the milk and cream in a bowl, and mix them together until well combined. Use a whisk to mix in the sugar. Continue to whisk for about 4 minutes until the sugar dissolves. Mix in the vanilla extract. Then mix in the orange juice. Finally whisk in the vodka.

✦ Pour the ingredients into the canister, follow the instructions above to set up your ice cream maker, and let it churn for 25 minutes.

✦ Serve immediately.

"Adults Old Fashioned" Ice Cream

This ice cream has the subtle flavor of an old fashioned thanks to whiskey and bitters. Try using rye whiskey for a slightly different flavor.

Prep Time: 2 Hours 50 Minutes
Servings: 6

INGREDIENTS
2 cups heavy cream
1 cup milk
3/4 cup sugar
1 tablespoon vanilla extract
3 tablespoons whiskey
1 dash of bitters

DIRECTIONS

- Place the milk and cream in a bowl, and mix them together until well combined. Use a whisk to mix in the sugar. Continue to whisk for about 4 minutes until the sugar dissolves. Then mix in the vanilla extract, whiskey, and bitters.

- Pour the ingredients into the canister, follow the instructions above to set up your ice cream maker, and let it churn for 25 minutes.

- Put the ice cream in an airtight container and place in the freezer for around 2 hours. Allow the ice cream to thaw for 15 minutes before serving.

"New York" Manhattan Ice Cream

This ice cream combines the flavors of whiskey, vermouth, and bitters like a real Manhattan. Add a cherry on top for the full Manhattan effect.

Prep Time: 2 Hours 50 Minutes
Servings: 6

INGREDIENTS
2 cups heavy cream
1 cup milk
3/4 cup sugar
1 tablespoon vanilla extract
3 tablespoons whiskey
1 tablespoon vermouth
1 dash of bitters

DIRECTIONS

- Place the milk and cream in a bowl, and mix them together until well combined. Use a whisk to mix in the sugar. Continue to whisk for about 4 minutes until the sugar dissolves. Then mix in the vanilla extract, whiskey, vermouth, and bitters.

- Pour the ingredients into the canister, follow the instructions above to set up your ice cream maker, and let it churn for 25 minutes.

- Put the ice cream in an airtight container and place in the freezer for around 2 hours. Allow the ice cream to thaw for 15 minutes before serving.

Creamy Kahlua Almond Delight Ice Cream

This ice cream has the sweet coffee flavor of Kahlua. The almonds give a good texture, and heighten the flavor of the Kahlua.

Prep Time: 2 Hours 50 Minutes
Servings: 6

INGREDIENTS
2 cups heavy cream
1 cup milk
3/4 cup sugar
1 teaspoon vanilla extract
3 tablespoons kahlua
3/4 cup chops almond

DIRECTIONS

- Place the milk and cream in a bowl, and mix them together until well combined. Use a whisk to mix in the sugar. Continue to whisk for about 4 minutes until the sugar dissolves. Then mix in the vanilla extract, kahlua.

- Pour the ingredients into the canister, follow the instructions above to set up your ice cream maker, and let it churn for 25 minutes. About 5 minutes before the ice cream is done churning add the almonds to your ice cream maker.

- Put the ice cream in an airtight container and place in the freezer for around 2 hours. Allow the ice cream to thaw for 15 minutes before serving.

"Tasty" Tequila Sunrise Gelato

This is the perfect gelato when you want something sweet and boozy. The orange juice and grenadine give this ice cream a nice fruity taste, and the tequila provides a kick.

Prep Time: 2 Hours 35 Minutes
Servings: 4-6

INGREDIENTS
1/2 cup heavy cream
2 cups milk
3/4 cup sugar
1/2 cup orange juice
1 teaspoon vanilla extract
3 tablespoons tequila
½ tablespoon grenadi

DIRECTIONS
- Place the milk and cream in a bowl, and mix them together until well combined. Use a whisk to mix in the sugar. Continue to whisk for about 4 minutes until the sugar dissolves. Then mix in the vanilla extract, orange juice, tequila and grenadine.

- Pour the ingredients into the canister, follow the instructions above to set up your ice cream maker, and let it churn for 25 minutes.

- Put the gelato in an airtight container and place in the freezer for up to 2 hours, until desired consistency is reached.

Samantha Kaine

Runnin' Rum And Coke Gelato

Now you can enjoy this sweet alcoholic beverage in a creamy frozen form. This gelato won't get you tipsy, but it will have you feeling good.

Prep Time: 2 Hours 50 Minutes
Servings: 4-6

INGREDIENTS
1/2 cup heavy cream
2 cups milk
3/4 cup sugar
1 teaspoon vanilla extract
3 tablespoons rum
3 cups coca cola (2, 12 ounce cans)

DIRECTIONS

✦ Pour the coke into a large skillet, and heat it on high heat until it comes to a boil. Allow the coke to cook for about another 15 or 20 minutes, until the coke reduces down to 1 cup of liquid. Let the liquid cool.

✦ Place the milk and cream in a bowl, and mix them together until well combined. Use a whisk to mix in the sugar. Continue to whisk for about 4 minutes until the sugar dissolves. Then mix in the vanilla extract, coke reduction, and rum.

✦ Pour the ingredients into the canister, follow the instructions above to set up your ice cream maker, and let it churn for 25 minutes.

✦ Put the gelato in an airtight container and place in the freezer for up to 2 hours, until desired consistency is reached.

Tropical Piña Colada Frozen Yogurt

Enjoy the tropical flavors of coconut and pineapple in this frozen yogurt. The rum gives a lovely sweetness and depth of flavor.

Prep Time: 2 Hours 35 Minutes
Servings: 1 Quart

INGREDIENTS
1 quart container full-fat plain yogurt
¼ teaspoon salt
1 cup sugar
½ cup pineapple juice
1 drop coconut essence
2 teaspoons lime juice
1/4 cup shredded coconut
4 tablespoons rum

DIRECTIONS

✦ Place the yogurt in a bowl. Use a whisk to mix in the sugar and salt. Continue to whisk for about 4 minutes until the sugar dissolves. Then mix in the rum, pineapple juice, lime juice, and coconut essence.

✦ Pour all the ingredients into the canister and stir well, follow the instructions above to set up your ice cream maker, and let it churn for 25 minutes.

✦ Put the frozen yogurt in an airtight container and place in the freezer for at least 2 hours, until desired consistency is reached.

Lickin' Lime Daiquiri Frozen Yogurt

You may not think of olive oil as something that goes in dessert, but it adds a nice nutty flavor, and creamy texture. Make sure to use a high quality olive oil.

Prep Time: 2 Hours 35 Minutes
Servings: 1 Quart

INGREDIENTS
1 quart container full-fat plain yogurt
¼ teaspoon salt
1 cup sugar
1/3 cup lime juice
4 tablespoons rum

DIRECTIONS

✦ Place the yogurt in a bowl. Use a whisk to mix in the sugar and salt. Continue to whisk for about 4 minutes until the sugar dissolves. Then mix in the rum, and lime juice.

✦ Pour the ingredients into the canister, follow the instructions above to set up your ice cream maker, and let it churn for 25 minutes.

✦ Put the frozen yogurt in an airtight container and place in the freezer for at least 2 hours, until desired consistency is reached.

The Guinness Chocolate Milkshake

Guinness has a full rich flavor that goes well with the richness of the chocolate. The Guinness adds a little body to this already rich shake.

Prep Time: 25 Minutes
Servings: 6

INGREDIENTS
2 cups heavy cream
1 cup milk
3/4 cup sugar
3 tablespoons Guinness beer
4 ounces chopped semi-sweet chocolate

DIRECTIONS
+ Melt the chocolate, and let it cool for a bit.

+ Place the milk and cream in a bowl, and mix them together until well combined. Use a whisk to mix in the sugar. Continue to whisk for about 4 minutes until the sugar dissolves. Then mix in the chocolate and Guinness.

+ Pour all the ingredients into the canister and stir well, follow the instructions above to set up your ice cream maker, and let it churn for 10-15 minutes, until desired consistency is reached.

+ Serve immediately.

Sunrise Strawberry Daiquiri Milkshake

Take the flavor of this tropical drink home with you. The flavors are made even better by the creaminess of the ice cream.

Prep Time: 25 Minutes
Servings: 6

INGREDIENTS
2 cups heavy cream
1 cup milk
3/4 cup sugar
4 tablespoons rum
8 ounces strawberries

DIRECTIONS
- Puree the strawberries in a food processor or blender.

- Place the milk and cream in a bowl, and mix them together until well combined. Use a whisk to mix in the sugar. Continue to whisk for about 4 minutes until the sugar dissolves. Then mix in the rum, and strawberry puree.

- Pour the ingredients into the canister, follow the instructions above to set up your ice cream maker, and let it churn for 10-15 minutes, until desired consistency is reached.

- Serve immediately.

Honey Cucumber Basil Rum Sorbet

The mellow flavor of the cucumber allows the freshness of the basil, and the sweetness of the rum to shine through. It's a lovely refreshing dessert for adults.

Prep Time: 2 hours 35 Minutes
Servings: 8

INGREDIENTS
4 cups chopped cucumbers
½ cup basil
½ cup honey
4 tablespoons rum

DIRECTIONS

- Use a food processor or blender to puree all the ingredients until smooth.

- Pour the ingredients into the canister, follow the instructions above to set up your ice cream maker, and let it churn for 25-30 minutes.

- Place in an airtight container for up to 2 hours, until desired consistency is reached.

Did You Appreciate This Publication?
Here's What You Do Now…

If you were pleased with our book then you can **Go to Amazon where you purchased this book and leave us a review**! In the world of an author who writes books independently, your reviews are not only touching but important so that we know you like the material we have prepared for "YOU" our audience! So leave us a review…we would love to see that you enjoyed our book!

If for any reason that you were less than happy with your experience then send me an email at **feedback@HealthyLifestyleRecipes.org** and let me know how we can better your experience. We always come out with a few volumes of our books and will possibly be able to address some of your concerns. Do keep in mind that we strive to do our best to give you the highest quality of what "we the independent authors" pour our heart and tears into.

Again…I really appreciate your purchase and thank you for your many great reviews and comments! With a warm heart!

~ Enjoy, Yours Truly

"Samantha Kaine"

A Little About The Author

Samantha Kaine is a trained highly skilled, trained and self taught private gourmet chef that has enjoyed her craft in the kitchens of many celebrities and exclusive events of Southern California and the Bay Area. She enjoys crafting new recipes for an array of categories and writes recipes and books from her heart and soul to share with you! In her spare time she enjoys long walks on the beach and reading a good book with a good mix of ice cream!

Hope you enjoyed my book and may your tongue & taste buds be dazzled and delighted! ;)

Samantha... xoxo

Samantha Kaine

Want Free Books?
... Of Course You Do!

Our New Books Sent To Your Email Monthly

For our current readers...if you like receiving FREE Books to add to your collection, then this is for you! This is for promoting our material to our current members so you can review our new books and give us feed back when we launch new books we are publishing! This helps us determine how we can make our books better for YOU, our audience! Just go to the url below and leave your name and email. We will send you a complimentary book about once a month. And just an FYI...on the website we've posted a few videos for you here too...

The Waffle Cone Recipe

Yours FREE for signing up to Our List!

www.HealthyLifestyleRecipes.org/FreeBook2Review

149

Other Books We Highly Recommend!

This Hamilton Beach® Ice Cream book is Awesome! **If you are looking for amazing desserts that go great with ice cream then you should check out "Ceramic Titanium Cookbook by Sasha Hassler & Allison August!** There are many different desserts that can be made in this non-stick ceramic titanium fry pan. With over 99 different recipes you will become a large fan of this great amazon selling cookbook! Click the link below: **www.amazon.com/Ceramic-Titanium-Cookbook-Delicious-Nutritious/dp/1545047995**

A second must have book that we highly recommend is our cuisinart 3-in-1 burger press cookbook! "MONSTER BURGER RECIPES!" This book is packed with some amazing ways to "burger your burgers!" Over 99 reasons to be the life of the party and control those bragging rights. After you try some of these "mile high" burgers you will never go back to the old way it was done in the past! So check this book out for yourself and grab one for your friends! It makes a great gift and even a better surprise!: link below!
www.Amazon.Com/Cuisinart-Burger-Press-Cookbook-Entertainment/Dp/1539557685

A Third Classic Book That We Highly Recommend Is Our Presto Electric Skillet Cookbook! You Can **Do The "Electric Slide"** With These Recipes Because They Are Nonstick And Slide Around In The Pan! This Book Will Show You How To Cut That Electric Bill In Half By Turning On That Electric Skillet And Whipping Up Some Of Those Savory Delicious Meals That Are Featured In This Easy To Make Recipe Book. We.Ve Got You Covered On All Types Of Meals You Can Make With This Skillet. This Recipe Book Will Show You How To: Stir Fry, Sauté, Bake, Warm And Even Whip Up Some Of The Most Delicious Desserts, "Just Like Grandma Used To Make!" Just Check It Out!
www.Amazon.Com/Our-Presto-Electric-Skillet-Cookbook-Ebook/Dp/B01N46QL1T

Recipe Notes

Recipe Notes

Printed in Great Britain
by Amazon